Universal Design for Learning in the Early Childhood Classroom

Universal Design for Learning in the Early Childhood Classroom focuses on proactively designing PreK through Grade 3 classroom environments, instruction, and assessments that are flexible enough to ensure that teachers can accommodate the needs of all the students in their classrooms. Typically developing students, gifted students, students who are impacted by poverty, children who speak multiple languages or have a home language that is different than the classroom language, and students with identified or potential developmental or learning disabilities are all covered within this highly practical, easy-to-use guide to UDL in the early years.

Pamela Brillante, Ed.D. is an Assistant Professor in the Department of Special Education and Professional Counseling at The William Paterson University of New Jersey with specialties in early childhood inclusive practices and disability studies.

Karen Nemeth, Ed.M. is an author, speaker, and consultant with expertise in first and second language development who founded Language Castle LLC.

D1601685

Other Eye On Education Books
Available from Routledge
(www.routledge.com/eyeoneducation)

Universal Design for Learning in the Early Childhood Classroom

Teaching Children of all Languages, Cultures, and Abilities, Birth – 8 Years

Pamela Brillante and Karen Nemeth

Routledge
Taylor & Francis Group

NEW YORK AND LONDON

First published 2018
by Routledge
711 Third Avenue, New York, NY 10017

and by Routledge
2 Park Square, Milton Park, Abingdon, Oxon, OX14 4RN

Routledge is an imprint of the Taylor & Francis Group, an informa business

© 2018 Taylor & Francis

The right of Pamela Brillante and Karen Nemeth to be identified as authors of this work has been asserted by them in accordance with sections 77 and 78 of the Copyright, Designs and Patents Act 1988.

Library of Congress Cataloging-in-Publication Data
A catalog record for this book has been requested

ISBN: 978-1-138-65512-6 (hbk)
ISBN: 978-1-138-65513-3 (pbk)
ISBN: 978-1-315-62273-6 (ebk)

Typeset in Palatino
by Swales & Willis Ltd, Exeter, Devon, UK

Contents

Meet the Authors

Pamela Brillante, Ed.D. joined many of the women in her family in public school teaching, finding her true passion in an early childhood special education classroom. Her career has taken her into the higher education classroom preparing the next generation of teachers at the William Paterson University of New Jersey. In addition to her work at the university, she continues to work as a consultant in public school classrooms, helping schools and teachers develop high quality inclusive programs and practices. Pam is an active member of NAEYC, serving as a consulting editor, and is the author of numerous journal articles and the book *The Essentials: Supporting Young Children with Disabilities in the Classroom.*

Karen Nemeth, Ed.M. started her consulting practice and her resources website, www.languagecastle.com, in 2009. Her mission has been to create resources, consult with programs, and provide professional development to improve early education experiences for young children from diverse backgrounds. She has written more than ten books, including *Young Dual Language Learners: A Guide for PreK–3 Leaders*, as well as many articles. She has worked to build connections across the disciplines that are involved in the education of young dual language learners and has served as consulting editor and Affiliate Advisory Council member of NAEYC, Steering Committee Representative for TESOL's Elementary Education Interest Section, and co-chair of NABE's Early Childhood Special Interest Group. She has worked with schools, organizations, and government agencies to develop guidance and supports to elevate practices for DLLs and their families in early care and education. In 2017, she was honored with the President's Award for leadership in the field by New Jersey's NJTESOL/NJBE organization.

1

Welcome to This Book and How to Use It

Schools Are Changing—What Does That Mean to a Teacher?

The field of early childhood education is changing in extraordinary ways. Expectations of teachers are expanding. Academic practices that were part of first grade are now appearing in kindergarten or even preschool. Parents are more engaged. Outcomes and accountability are top priorities for district administrators and state governments.

Student populations are becoming more diverse and programs are becoming more inclusive. General education teachers have become responsible for the educational progress of all children in the classroom, including children who may not speak the same language as the teacher and the other students in the class, and children who have identified disabilities or may have learning disabilities that the teacher uncovers.

Learning is a complex concept, and all children learn at different paces and in different ways. This makes how we provide instruction and how we assess what students know and can do a complicated undertaking. Focusing on developmentally appropriate practices (DAP) and remaining both flexible and observant is key. According to the position statement on DAP by the National Association for the Education of Young Children (NAEYC, 2009), the underlying element of DAP is intentionality. Teachers proactively and intentionally make decisions about environments, materials, and instruction that are flexible enough to be both challenging and achievable for every student.

Be Prepared

Successful early childhood teachers approach their work with openness and flexibility. They realize that a "one size fits all" mindset won't help them work effectively with the diverse students they encounter. Every child needs access to a developmentally appropriate early childhood education that meets their individual needs and helps them to participate and make progress toward the standards (Brillante, 2017). This is a high expectation, and now both teachers and administrators have to know more and do more to support and integrate programs from preK to third grade and beyond. State education departments, such as Maryland and New Jersey, are reflecting this high expectation by recommending Universal Design for Learning (UDL) in their regulations.

The purpose of this book is to help readers find the most effective and most achievable path to success in early childhood education in the face of all this change. You will learn about the overarching concepts of Universal Design and how to use the framework of Universal Design for Learning within the DAP approach, towards the goal of meeting the needs of all young children in the early childhood classroom.

The advantage of the universally designed approach is that it shifts the focus away from reacting to problems by making adaptations. It focuses more on proactively designing the classroom to make sure all students will be able to get what they need right from the start. Universally designed strategies do not interfere with typical children in any way. So, for example, an older school may be built so the only way to get into the front of the building is stairs. A child who uses a wheelchair needs a ramp to be able to get into the building-but, if we stop to think about it, every child can use a ramp to get into the building! In fact, a recent review of research found that "Implementing UDL in education is a promising solution to minimise learning barriers" (Al-Azawei, Serenelli, & Lundqvist, 2016, p. 51). With UDL strategies, educators can make it possible for each and every child to be the best he can be.

1. *Universal Design for Learning (UDL)* is a framework that helps all teachers in all classrooms adapt to meet the needs of each individual child. While the Center for Applied Special Technology (CAST) has started a great movement to use this approach for children with disabilities, we are expanding the framework to work with young children with varying needs.

2. *Developmentally Appropriate Practice (DAP)* is an approach that focuses on supporting the learning of each individual young child according to his or her interests and level of development. Materials from the NAEYC list the three key considerations of DAP as knowing about child development and learning, knowing what is individually appropriate, and knowing what

is culturally appropriate. In collaboration with the Council for Exceptional Children Division for Early Childhood, NAEYC made this key recommendation regarding early childhood curriculum: "To benefit all children, including those with disabilities and developmental delays, it is important to implement an integrated, developmentally appropriate, universally designed curriculum framework that is flexible, comprehensive, and linked to assessment and program evaluation activities" (Division for Early Childhood [DEC], 2007, p. 3).

3. *DECAL* is a guide for preparing all teachers to meet the needs of children with Different Experiences, Cultures, Abilities, and Languages as a way to focus professional learning and preparation (Nemeth, Brillante, & Mullen, 2017):

   ◆ **Experiences** (family income, home literacy practices, stress and trauma, safe environments, health and physical development supports, early care and education, etc.)
   ◆ **Culture** (family, community, home country, traditions)
   ◆ **Abilities** (gifted, individual learning strengths/abilities/potentials, identified or potential disabilities, mental health issues)
   ◆ **Languages** (frequently occurring or rare languages, multiple languages).

Together, these three components fit perfectly to create the most advanced approach to early childhood education for the diverse, inclusive classrooms of today. We know teachers face many challenges in this complex world, so our goal is to weave together the elements of

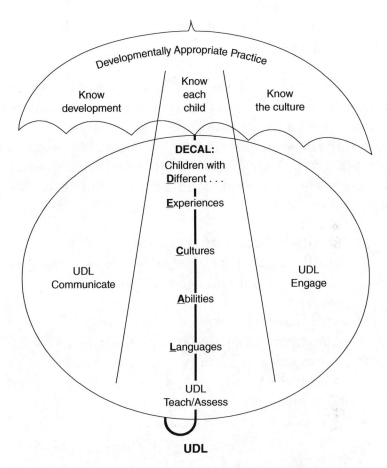

Figure 1.1 Component Crosswalk for Universal Design for Learning in Early Childhood Education

that complexity and provide simple, practical strategies that can be used in any program, with any curriculum, to achieve success for all young children. We will be breaking down the boundaries between different specialties. Teachers don't need to be experts in all categories of education, but they can be very effective if they know how to combine the best strategies from each category. That is what you will find in this book.

What Teachers Need to Know and Be Able to Do in Schools of the Future

The chapters of this book will help readers to provide the kind of flexible, responsive, and rigorous educational experience that every child needs to succeed. To create your learning goals for reading this book, check off the items that you want to learn more about. To succeed in diverse early childhood education, every teacher will need to know

- ◆ how first and second languages develop
- ◆ how the brain of a young child learns, processes information, and manages emotions and behavior
- ◆ evidence of what works to facilitate communication across potential barriers
- ◆ best practices for scaffolding early learning
- ◆ principles of developmentally, linguistically, and culturally appropriate assessments
- ◆ how culture impacts learning
- ◆ how to teach young children with varying needs, including:
    - o Children with disabilities or children with individual abilities (not "special needs")
    - o Children who are dual language learners or DLLs (instead of English language learners, ELLs)
    - o Children from low income, high stress, or unstable housing experiences (rather than "poor children" or "high-risk children")
    - o Children with individual cultural backgrounds (rather than Asians or Hispanics).

And teachers will need to be able to

- conduct and record accurate, objective observations
- conduct and interpret appropriate assessments
- adapt communication strategies
- adapt lesson plans
- adapt teaching practices to respond to each child's needs
- design classroom space to make learning accessible to all
- build relationships with diverse families
- find, create, and modify classroom materials to meet the needs of all students
- use technology in appropriate ways to make learning accessible and relatable for students of all languages, cultures and abilities.

Can one teacher do all of these things? Yes! The UDL framework will help. The UDL framework has three key principles: supporting multiple means of representation, employing multiple means of action and expression to teach, and connecting children and families using multiple means of engagement. When you read a professional development article or book, your first question may be, "What does this mean to me as a teacher?" Each chapter of this book will begin with an answer to that question according to those UDL principles.

Special Features in This Book

a. "What it means to a teacher"—You will start with the answer and then find details to support that answer as you read through the chapter;

b. Questions in each chapter to support a book study group or professional learning community discussion;

c. Illustrations, photos, diagrams, tables, and planning charts to enhance learning;

d. Teacher self-assessment checklists to help the reader actively engage with content by checking where they are and looking for what they need in the chapter;

e. A section at the end of the book with guidance for administrators and professional development providers;

f. Index;

g. References;

h. Resources.

Now, we invite you to join us on a journey toward a brighter future for all children and for all early childhood educators!

2

Using UDL as a Framework

Providing Multiple Means of Representation

What Does This Mean to a Teacher?

Children perceive and understand information in many different ways, and the way that information is presented to them matters. Learning happens when the information is presented in ways that children can understand and connect to previous learning and experiences. When children have different languages or cultural interaction styles or language abilities, teachers must be more effective in using a variety of communication tools and update their classroom environment to focus on easy, authentic communication that can work for all children.

Guided Questions

- How do you routinely present information to the students in your classroom? Is it always with visuals? Do you always talk about the topic? How many ways do you present the same information?

◆ When do you find it most challenging to communicate with the children in your group?

◆ What kind of technology are you most comfortable using that could help you establish multiple means of representation in your classroom?

◆ Take a closer look at the items on display in your classroom. How are you presenting information that you want your children to know? Which items are really used to facilitate communication? Which are rarely or never discussed?

Multiple Means of Representation—Classroom Design

The makeup of the learning environment is a key aspect to any early childhood classroom. Young children learn through play, and thinking about changes we can make to the design of play centers and play materials is essential when we think about Universal Design in the early childhood classroom. Learning spaces communicate so much to children, families, and professionals. The way a space is designed can convey the level of independence expected of children by offering more or fewer challenges. Displays and materials also convey to families how welcome they are and what expectations the program has of them.

The UDL framework gives you powerful guidance about re-envisioning your classroom to communicate the messages you think are important in many different ways. If you want to foster resourceful, competent, and knowledgeable learners, you can change the classroom environment to make learning accessible and relatable to each child and all children with the following strategies.

Spaces can only do so much to develop a child's sense of place and sense of belonging. Proactive planning of spaces, routines, and activities take time and effort. UDL can be this framework for the proactive planning of spaces, routines, and activities. We need to construct the social and physical environment with the realization that what we do determines the ways in which children interact and participate.

DECAL: Classroom Design to Meet the Needs of Children from Different Experiences

Some children enter school with unpredictable backgrounds including limited home literacy practices, unstable home environments, or traumatic events. You can make proactive changes in the classroom to be more responsive to their needs.

> Ask yourself: How can I look at my environment through the eyes of a child who has not had any experience with a stable school or home?

Teacher Tips!

◆ For a child with a transient lifestyle, having a safe place to keep personal belongings can be very helpful to keep them feeling secure and able to focus on learning. Provide a cubby that can be locked or similar space for all children to ensure the needs of the unsure children are met.

(continued)

(continued)

- ◆ For children who experience poverty, access to learning at school may be interrupted by hunger, poor hygiene, or lack of basic necessities. Keep a collection of toothbrushes, socks, hats, mittens, snacks, and other items that might be needed. Don't ask questions; just make these items available for all children.
- ◆ Check your books, displays, and games to be sure there are items that are relatable for each child. Some children may not have the experiences that other children have had, so their prior knowledge may be different. Stories about farms should be balanced with stories about city life. The dramatic play area could have items representing shopping at stores as well as thrift shops. A class lending library can ensure that all families have home literacy materials regardless of their incomes.
- ◆ Many children may not have experiences with whole groups of children, so they may not understand the signs and symbols that teachers use to teach classroom routines. Explicitly teaching these routines and symbols may be needed to understand and interpret.
- ◆ Access to the internet and technology resources is important, as it can reduce the digital divide and help all students grow up with experiences they will need for future educational and career success.
- ◆ Look for more detailed suggestions in the appendix of this book!

DECAL: Classroom Design to Meet the Needs of Children from Different Cultures

Children learn best in environments with materials they can relate to.

> Look around your room for cultural connections. Are you representing the culture of each child in the classroom?

Of course, it is important to avoid stereotypes, but that can leave some classrooms looking like there is no culture at all. Authentic connections with a child's culture help the child perceive the information you want to teach more easily and are best gathered with the help of their families. When you make a poster using photos sent in by the families of the children, you help to build connections and comprehension that can't happen as well with purchased "multicultural" posters. The environment should reflect the traditions, celebrations, and activities that are familiar to each child every day, not just during token "multicultural weeks" or designated months.

Teacher Tips!

- ◆ Learn words and phrases of the children's home language to help present new information in many different ways.
- ◆ Collect culturally relevant play and learning materials through local flea markets, yard sales and thrift shops, families, and cultural organizations that can build prior knowledge or be a visual/tactile example.

(continued)

(continued)

◆ Learn as much as you can about the culture of each child that is meaningful to them. Magazines, newspapers, and catalogs from different countries can help you develop a better understanding so you can make sure you are making the correct connections for this child.

DECAL: Classroom Design to Meet the Needs of Children with Different Abilities

The environment can support access for all children, both inside and outside, with careful planning.

How accessible is the environment for children with different abilities? Can all children access the room and participate in activities no matter what their ability level, visual or hearing needs, or physical challenges?

The goal of preparing an environment for all children is to foster independence wherever possible. Installing a ramp so a child with limited mobility can get into the classroom along with his peers is a better option than employing an aide to carry the child into the classroom. The addition of adaptations like ramps, braille, or sign language can make all the difference between dependence and independence for some children. Often, this type of planning means that there are options with varying levels of challenge, so each child gets the experience he or she needs.

Independence is key for many children with differing abilities. If you find yourself helping a child with the same routine repeatedly, chances are it is time to reconsider that routine. Safety is an important consideration, but ensuring safety does not mean coddling children to protect them from everything. Four-year-old children can learn to cut with knives. Provide plastic knives so all children get the fine motor practice of cutting food or dough, but the children with lower dexterity, or children who have vision impairments, are not in danger of cutting themselves.

Teacher Tips!

- ◆ Look at the physical space from the child's perspective. Make sure everything is in reach of the children so they can get materials or toys and put them away on their own. Independence is key!
- ◆ Use outdoor play equipment that encourages climbing, swinging, and hanging but with enough space so children with visual disabilities or physical disabilities can participate safely.
- ◆ Add visual cues in the environment to assist children with hearing impairments participate and be engaged with peers and materials while maintaining independence. Using a clapping sequence to signal clean up is not effective for them—but turning on and off the lights would be. The best choice is to do both things!

(continued)

(continued)

◆ Include tactile cues, such as braille letters or different textures to classroom labels, to support children with visual impairments.

◆ Ask scout troops or college groups to design adaptations for furniture and equipment.

Too often, individuals with disabilities are over-protected by parents and teachers, and, therefore, never get the opportunity to experience the consequences of poor choices. Risk taking provides individuals with disabilities different learning opportunities and new experiences within their environment so that they may test their own limits and discover capabilities they may not have known they had (Opportunity for Independence, 2011). Allowing individuals with disabilities to take risks and to move toward greater independence is an essential component of becoming an adult. It is also important to find that balance that supports risk taking without real danger.

DECAL: Classroom Design to Meet the Needs of Children from Different Languages

All young children need to see evidence of their home language or languages in their school environment. Research has shown that young children retain some information in their home language even if they are progressing well in the use of English. Continuing to connect with their prior knowledge in their home language actually supports their developing proficiency in English. Young children with different language backgrounds also benefit from visual cues in the environment to help them understand what is happening in English. These cues are also helpful for children with language or cognitive delays, as well.

> Can you identify the language needs of each child in your class? Knowing this information will assist you in updating the environment appropriately.

For maximum benefit, environmental print must be meaningful and useful in the classroom. Environmental print that no one ever reads or talks about is just like wallpaper in the background. Too much print can create an unsettling level of clutter that reduces language use and comprehension. The goal should be to reduce the visual stimuli in the classroom and change it often, so you can be sure what is visible really contributes to communication between adults and children and peer to peer.

Teacher Tips!

◆ Classroom labels should be reconsidered. Placing a label on the chair that says "chair" or a label over the bookshelf that says "library area" won't really help any child communicate. But, a label in the science area with pictures showing the steps children should use to explore some new materials would enable children with different languages or different language abilities to independently participate in science explorations. Some programs add QR codes

(continued)

(continued)

to classroom labels that children can scan with a handheld device to hear the words pronounced in their language and/or English.

◆ A clear picture schedule should be on the wall of every classroom to enable each child to feel secure in knowing what is expected and what will happen next.

◆ A poster with welcoming words or greetings in different languages can be an asset at the beginning of the year, but you can advance language learning by changing that poster to add new words for all the children and adults to learn throughout the year. If the same "hello" poster is left in place all year, it, too, will become like wallpaper.

◆ As school choice becomes an increasingly important topic, remember that families get their first impression of your school before they even enter the building. Are different languages available on the school website or on flyers and signs?

◆ The idea of a picture exchange communication system (PECS) comes from special education, but the truth is, communication by pointing to relevant pictures is a strategy that can help many children communicate across language barriers.

◆ Invite family members to be recorded as they walk around the classroom identifying different areas and items in their home languages. These videos can help teachers learn key words in the home languages of the children and can help children gain a better

> understanding of the components of their daily classroom experience.
>
> ◆ Some schools post videos on their website or Facebook page to show families about the routines of the school. These videos can help families who don't speak English to prepare their child for fire drills, lunchroom procedures, and other important routines.
>
> ◆ Open conversation at snack time so children may express opinions and disagree strongly, but do not allow name-calling.
>
> ◆ Peers are also part of the educational environment. Group children with the same language so they have plenty of opportunities to play and interact in their home language during the day, and they can help each other learn words in the new language as well.

Multiple Means of Representation—Learning Materials

DECAL: Learning Materials That Support Children from Different Experiences

Classroom materials that reflect a child's early experiences are important for several reasons. Not only do they help the child relate new information to their experiences, but they also validate the child's experience and convey the message that all children are valuable regardless of their family income, housing situation, or any other experience. It is also important to bring in elements that will expose children to information and activities they might not otherwise be able to experience. For example, many books, songs, and puzzles focus on farm animals. For city children, this is not a very relatable topic. That doesn't mean all references to farms should be eliminated. Instead, consider shifting the balance so there are more materials that connect to the children's current environment and just a few exposures to information about farms.

Assess the images and messages found in the books, puzzles, games, toys, music, dramatic play, and other learning materials in your classroom to see if they can make every child's experience part of the school day.

Teacher Tips!

◆ Create class books using photos of the children's actual homes, neighborhoods, and the school community so children can more easily perceive the meaning. Think about places the children go such as the grocery store, food bank, park, zoo, homeless shelter, bank, welfare office, clinic, grange center, veterinarian, county fair, street festival, and so on.

◆ Use family photos glued to boxes and blocks to make relatable people in the block or table toy area.

◆ In the small toy or manipulatives area, replace meaningless plastic items with real items that children see at home in order to add context and access prior knowledge. When you teach sorting with a collection of socks, children see the same items at home and can extend their learning in ways that don't happen with plastic school supplies.

DECAL: Learning Materials That Support Children from Different Cultures

A child's culture is mostly about his own home, family, traditions, and activities. Some exposure to the culture of his home country can be interesting, but is not always relatable for a young child. For example, we think of baseball as the sport that represents American culture, but if a child lives with a family of avid soccer fans, then soccer is culturally relevant for that child more than baseball. The best way to get to know what will make sense to the child is to ask his family.

> Ask each family about their celebrations, favorite meals, how they spend time together, music they listen to, traditions, and the toys/songs/games they remember from their own childhood so you can incorporate these things throughout the school environment.

update survey?

It is important to get to know each family and to avoid making assumptions about their culture based on their appearance or their name. Once you have more information, you can build cultural connections into all areas of the classroom and outdoor area.

Teacher Tips!

◆ Cultures can be represented in the types of plants and herbs grown in the school garden.
◆ Traditional children's songs from other countries can be nice, but so can an afternoon spent learning some salsa dance steps or creating a rap about sharing with friends.

(continued)

(continued)

◆ Ask families to take pictures of their child's plate at dinner and use the images to create class books or laminate them to serve as pretend food in the dramatic play area. Families can also send in empty food containers that can be cleaned and used here, too.

◆ Visit thrift stores to collect dress-up items rather than ordering inauthentic items from catalogs. Look for sports jerseys representing children's favorite teams, or uniforms from different professions, for example. A migrant/seasonal Head Start program might include bags used in harvesting crops. A school in a coastal town might include fishing equipment. An Alaskan program might have snowshoes.

◆ If your curriculum provides required reading books, create supplemental materials that support the vocabulary and topics in those books that provide additional images that are culturally relevant to use as puzzles or memory game pieces.

◆ Build a partnership with the local children's librarian. Librarians have access to a wide range of catalogs and resources that can help to provide children's books as well as music, videos, and adult resources representing different cultures such as cookbooks or travel books.

DECAL: Learning Materials That Support Children with Different Abilities

Materials should be available so that children with different intellectual and physical abilities can have access to learning the same content in different ways. The focus does not have to be about a high or low level; instead, make sure the children have access to the same information through multiple avenues.

> Look at the materials in your classroom from the perspective of a child who has trouble understanding things or communicating. How can adaptations to materials help each child participate at his or her own level?

Teacher Tips!

◆ Group books by topic, so each group has board books, picture books, and higher level books, so children with different abilities can access multiple books with the same content but at different levels.

◆ Instead of games with thin cards that are hard to pick up, paste the cards onto pieces of thick cardboard or foam board for easy handling.

◆ Understand that for some students, there may be some missing knowledge or limited experiential background, so add as much of that to the classroom as you can.

DECAL: Learning Materials That Support Children from Different Languages

All young children benefit from opportunities to learn and practice their home language. When children grow up with one or more languages in addition to English, classroom materials can help provide the needed supports even if the teacher doesn't speak every child's language. Some items can be purchased in different languages or borrowed from the library. When these options are not available, you can have some of your existing materials translated. Always be cautious about any translation, whether it is from the internet or another person, and have all translations checked by at least one other person. Some online translation services or apps are meant for use by adult travelers or for business use. Even though their translations may be accurate, they may use forms that are not familiar to children. Some words and phrases do not translate well. For example, in the U.S., it is common for early childhood educators to say "clean up time" when they want children to put away toys. In other countries, the term "clean up" refers to washing things, and the preferred term equates more to "tidy up." This could confuse a child who is new to English.

When adding languages to materials in the classroom, be sure to choose words and phrases that children will use many times in meaningful conversations.

Teacher Tips!

- ◆ When adding languages to classroom labels and materials, use color coding so children and adults will know that each language has its own color. For example, if Korean is always green, you can put green stickers on the books that are in Korean and on CDs that have Korean music, too.
- ◆ Add stickers inside of books with key words translated into the language needed by the children—and include phonetic spelling so any adult or child can pronounce the word.

◆ Add more real items for math, science, and other manipulative activities. Dual language learners get a head start when working with familiar materials that they understand and know about. This is another reason to use socks for sorting games instead of meaningless plastic toys or cut-out shapes. Collect items from nature, from kitchens, sports, and so on.

◆ Be more intentional about choosing songs in different languages. Look for music with words that children can use in activities and interactions. Just because a song is available in another language doesn't mean it will teach children anything if they don't use the words outside of the song.

◆ Adding pictures to labels is a good way to support different languages, but be intentional with your choices. If you put a label on a chair with a picture of a chair but it is already on a real chair, does the picture add meaning? Maybe a picture of children pushing in their chairs or sitting in chairs to have a snack would provide more context to talk about.

◆ Menus from diverse restaurants in the dramatic play area can provide food-related words in different languages.

◆ Models of different alphabets should be available in the writing area.

◆ Plastic and magnetic letters are available in some languages other than English. If you

(continued)

(continued)

> need other characters, print them out and
> glue onto plastic sheets and add magnets.
> ◆ Give children access to brief videos
>   showing how to play a game or complete an
>   assignment with instructions in their home
>   language so they can then participate with
>   their peers.

Multiple Means of Representation—Technology and Digital Resources

DECAL: Technology and Digital Resources That Support Different Experiences

Technology is being used in many ways in today's schools. Many experts are concerned about "the digital divide" separating children with advantages from children who have little or no access to technology (Neuman & Celano, 2012). We want all children to grow up knowing how to use digital tools, and we also want all children to have access to the information and activities that are available with digital tools and internet access. These experiences don't have to be exactly the same, but the divide should not be wide enough to influence differences in school performance or career success. In early childhood education, the teacher has the responsibility for finding an appropriate balance.

What do you know about each family's use of and access to technology? How can you enhance these experiences for home and school?

Teacher Tips!

◆ Not all families have access to the internet, but most families have smartphones (Rideout & Katz, 2016). Help children learn to use handheld devices effectively to search for information on the internet, to use calculators, and to communicate and learn via text messages and videos.

◆ If your school has a computer lab, create programs that invite families and children to use these resources outside of school time to accomplish tasks and to learn together.

◆ Provide guidance to families to help them guide their child's technology use. Families with easy access may still not know what is best for young children.

◆ Get to know the availability of technology resources at local libraries, museums, and other organizations.

DECAL: Technology and Digital Resources That Support Children from Different Cultures

Online resources can help teachers and students understand different cultures, but when schools put severe limits on internet use, these resources may be out of reach. For example, YouTube can provide a great window on the world. You can find videos depicting many cultural practices, activities, and traditions. Of course, educators know they should proceed with caution.

What sources do you use to find information about the cultures of your children? Which of these sources are useful for your students?

Teacher Tips!

◆ The Bridging Refugee Youth and Children's Services website (www.brycs.org) provides information to help you understand the refugee conditions faced by families in different parts of the world.

◆ Digital pen pals can interact with each other via email or video chats to get to know how children live and learn in different countries.

◆ Also consider using video chats such as Google Hangouts or Skype to contact the relatives and friends of children in their home countries.

◆ Use digital photographs representing the culture of each child's family to make placemats, books, math activities, posters, and much more.

DECAL: Technology and Digital Resources That Support Children with Different Abilities

Technology offers amazing opportunities to enable children with different abilities to participate fully in school activities. Some software and hardware have been developed to compensate for specific disabilities, but they may be very expensive. There are many ways that technology can be used inexpensively to support different abilities, as well.

Before making a purchase, consider whether an app or device designed for people with disabilities is worth the cost or if the same function could be served by an app designed for general use.

Teacher Tips!

◆ Many augmentative and alternate communication systems can help young children with limited expressive language to communicate. You might also achieve the same goal by simply printing out digital photos and tacking them to a board.

◆ Look for apps that children can start and use independently without a lot of barriers to entry.

◆ Find software with multiple levels of play or learning so that each child can progress at their own pace. Look for scaffolded supports as well.

◆ Apps and software that provide voice-to-text functionality allow children to say answers to questions or tell stories when they are not yet able to type on small keys.

◆ Show children how to use the zoom-in features so they can make images larger when they are hard to see.

◆ Use apps that turn tablets into paddle switches to help children participate in games with peers.

◆ Handheld devices also give children access to voice commands and prompts so they can hear what other children are reading or learn how to perform new routines or games.

DECAL: Technology and Digital Resources That Support Children from Different Languages

The number of languages found in early childhood classrooms can be overwhelming. A teacher may collect materials in several languages during one school year, only to find those children move on and her class is filled with different languages the following year. Technology helps teachers be more responsive to changing or challenging language needs. It is always important to double check translations and meanings to be sure you are providing resources that are appropriate for young children.

Which languages are being underserved in your classroom? How might technology enable you to improve those language supports?

Teacher Tips!

◆ Collaborate with other teachers or join online professional learning networks to find out about new options for supporting different languages using digital resources.

◆ Look for e-books and apps with multiple language options so children can both read and hear stories in different languages.

◆ Multilingual websites with digital stories can be found at www.icdlbooks.org and www. TumbleBooks.com.

◆ Apps with learning games that do not depend on language make learning accessible to children from any language. Find examples at www.tocaboca.com.

- ◆ Access online stores to search for books and music in many languages. Even if you don't buy all of them, you can create a list for the librarian or as a wish list for donations.
- ◆ Download the Google Translate app onto your tablet, and use the camera to scan printed documents and change the words to another language. Google Translate Online allows you to both see and hear translated words pronounced.
- ◆ With book making apps such as My Story, children can draw, type, fingerspell, and illustrate their own stories and include recorded voice narration in any language.

3

Using UDL as a Framework

Providing Multiple Means of Action and Expression

What Does This Mean to a Teacher?

Children participate in activities and demonstrate what they know in the classroom in many different ways. Providing multiple means of action and expression can help children with differing needs, such as language barriers, physical disabilities, and even impulse control issues, have the options they need to be able to participate and play with the materials in the environment in order to learn new skills and be able to demonstrate what they know.

Guided Questions

◆ Which centers in your classroom are well used by the children and which centers are ignored by the children? Do children stay longer at certain centers and have more complex play with those materials? Do specific children seem to ignore a particular center?

◆ How are the children in your group expressing what they know and can do during activities? Which children are the most challenging for you to know what they can do or interpret what they are trying to show/tell you? What contributes to this challenge?

◆ When you step back and watch the children in child-directed activities, what are they doing? How are they playing and planning what to do? Are they using the skills and knowledge you have taught them in teacher-directed activities? What other skills are they using?

Core Considerations of DAP for Action and Expression

Understanding children as individuals helps us provide meaningful, relevant, and respectful learning experiences in the classroom. The NAEYC position statement on DAP focuses on three primary, or core, considerations for teachers:

1. *Knowing about child development and learning.* It is important for every teacher to understand the stages and progression of typical development for the children in their class, for all the learning domains. This knowledge, based on years of research, helps teachers design experiences and instruction that are best for each child's learning and development. Whether a teacher is new to the field or is being reassigned from an older grade, specific understanding of the children in each new class will be needed to support effective means of action and expression for each child.

2. *Knowing what is individually appropriate.* All children are different and many have different experiences, cultures, abilities, and languages that teachers need to take into consideration when they are designing instruction and assessments. By getting to know the children both in and out of the classroom, we can learn about them developmentally, and watching them play and interact with peers helps us to get to know their preferences and interests. Allowing each child to receive and express learning in ways that are individually appropriate is essential to both DAP and the UDL framework.

3. *Knowing what is culturally important.* Children cannot be understood in isolation but rather as a part of an interconnected and interdependent family system. We must make an effort to get to know the children's families on a deeper level. Understanding the values, expectations, and cultural factors that shape each child's life at home and in their communities is necessary for effective action and expression in early education (National Association for the Education of Young Children, 2009).

Executive Function Skills

Another key aspect of the action/expression part of the UDL framework is the development of the self-regulation skills needed for children to be active learners and to be able to plan and execute tasks on their own. As a group, these skills are known as executive function, which becomes a complete process of setting a goal (like building a large complex structure in the block area), and then having the ability to organize their ideas and the resources they have to be able to follow through to achieve that goal as independently as possible. Can the child persist at the task? Can she keep in mind the steps her task will take? Can she adapt when a step does not go as planned? The ability to organize ideas is a precursor to being able to express the depth of knowledge and understanding of concepts. When children exhibit executive function skills, teachers are able to have a much more accurate assessment of their knowledge and skills no matter what way they express them (NAEYC, 2009).

Action and Expression in the Early Childhood Classroom

Ways to Make Content Accessible to Children: DECAL in the Classroom

Our own understanding of curriculum as a vehicle for learning has to become broader. While some curricula may have an end concept or skill in mind that all children should have at the end of a school year or a specific age – *how* we get there can be very different from child to child. We are all headed to the same destination, but the vehicles we are in and the roads we take are going to be different for many children.

Unknowingly or not, the teaching practices used in the classroom reflect the adult's belief about each child and whether every child is considered an equal and valued member of the classroom (Brillante, 2017). To proactively design instruction for all children from a common curriculum, teachers must first understand the needs, strengths, and preferences of each child, so they can design the classroom, formal instruction, and informal learning opportunities so that all the children can participate and learn at the same time.

To implement the action/expression aspect of UDL when we are talking about children with different experiences, cultures, abilities and languages, the biggest change needs to come from the teacher by changing the way they design instruction, organize the classroom, and conduct assessments (Burgstahler, 2008). The most common, and effective, classroom practices support differentiation so they can be used with all children, and the UDL framework makes that possible. The following strategies show how to establish practices using the action/expression principle of the UDL framework.

The Basics for Every Young Child: Action
- ◆ Provide some options for physical action/active participation.
- ◆ Design activities with different ways to do things and different ways for children to participate and respond.

The Basics for Every Young Child: Expression
- ◆ Provide multiple options and ways for every child to communicate with everyone in the classroom.
- ◆ Support the child only as needed so they become independent.

The Basics for Every Young Child: Executive Function
- ◆ Teach the child to set their own goals and decide how they are going to accomplish tasks.
- ◆ Support planning and strategy development to promote independence.

The Basics of Active Learning

◆ Each child has the ability or an individualized strategy to communicate with others in the classroom (gestural, spoken, and written; words, sounds, and images; in person and electronic).

◆ Each child has the appropriate level of support from the teacher, other adults, and peers, and can offer support to others.

The Basics of Routines and Schedules

◆ Children learn best when they understand and follow a consistent schedule each day. The routines and schedule are taught to the child in a way they understand and can predict.

◆ There is an emphasis on planning most of the day with small groups and individualized activities, keeping whole group work to a very small minimum. This balance should be based on each individual child's needs at the time. There is no one-size-fits-all schedule.

◆ There is a balance of special activities that deviate from the routine schedule of the classroom, but the children are prepared for these changes and are not required to go if they do not want to.

The Basics of Ongoing Assessment

◆ Assessment is both formal and informal, and builds on the child's prior knowledge and skills.

◆ Assessment is embedded within both curricular and real-life activities and is not done in isolation.

◆ Assessment is focused on how the child uses the skills and knowledge within everyday activities and routines, not in a staged setting or event.

◆ Assessment is both linguistically and culturally appropriate for each child.

Let's look at how you can think about instruction and materials through the lens of making them accessible and appropriate for children from the perspective of DECAL.

Multiple Means of Action and Expression—Active Learning

Active learning happens when each child has the opportunity to engage with different materials, actions, and events. It is important for children to have the opportunity to make choices and decisions about themselves and what they want to do and, when appropriate, be part of the decision making when helping the group decide what they will do.

DECAL: Active Learning for Children from Different Experiences

Teachers need to understand the different experiences a child has had before coming into their classroom. Have they had the same access to the materials (i.e., computers, pretend play toys) as other children in the classroom? Do they need different opportunities to explore the items on a basic level that the other children do not need? In some cases, teachers may have to provide direct instruction on how things work and how to play with them in order for the child to be able to learn and express what they know.

Which classroom materials are new to your students? How are you going to teach them what these things are and how they are used?

Teacher Tips!

◆ Give the children access and time with materials they may not have at home or they may not be familiar with at all. Experiences are key to much knowledge, and they may not have had the opportunity to have the same experiences as everyone else in the class.

◆ Provide direct instruction to fill some of the gaps in experiences.

◆ Every child has strengths and abilities that can be incorporated in plans for play experiences.

◆ Be conscious of the use of food as an instructional material (dried rice or beans in a sand table, or using an apple with tempera paint on it to make artwork). It can be considered disrespectful to use food in that way if a child goes hungry at dinnertime or over the weekend. Be conscious of your choices and of the children's experiences.

◆ Check your own definition of "fair." Some children who do not have items like you have in your class may need extra time with those materials to catch up to the experiences of other children. Fair should mean that everyone gets what they need.

DECAL: Active Learning for Children from Different Cultures

Different cultures may have different views on teachers, schools, and education in general. Some families do not understand the use of project-based learning, play, and active learning when children investigate problems, so the children may appear hesitant to participate in group work (Cambridge International, 2015). Have culturally appropriate options for students when necessary.

What cultural views could the families in your class have about teachers and schools? You may have to investigate this yourself, but always double check to make sure it is true for the families in your class.

Teacher Tips!

- ◆ Be flexible with your own teaching practices. It really is OK to be outside of the box sometimes with the whole group, or with just selected children. Not everyone has to do things the same way.
- ◆ Incorporate some of the cultural traditions about the children that you have learned, or work with the families to learn more.
- ◆ Let children take the lead and show you what they know in any way they feel comfortable. In fact, encourage that.

DECAL: Active Learning for Children with Different Abilities

Children with different abilities have a right to have access to the same education as their same-age peers. The content and standards are the same for everyone, but the ways in which children with differing abilities access the content and demonstrate their knowledge is what needs to change. Instructional strategies for teaching students with varying abilities must by adapted and modified in order to support the child to have access to and actively participate in high-quality experiences and make progress toward developmentally appropriate goals (Brillante, 2017). In addition, with children who are gifted or have strengths in specific areas, there is always the need for a solid foundation in all areas in order for them to be able to explore at a higher level and bring a deeper meaning to their learning.

All children, and particularly children with disabilities, need to actively participate in instruction in order to learn. The Division of Early Childhood (DEC) (2007) recommended using the framework of UDL in order to promote positive outcomes for children with disabilities, including promoting active engagement and learning, as well as individualizing and adapting practices for each child based on ongoing data. Young children who are gifted are naturally curious children who plunge into new activities or situations quickly and positively and tend to initiate their own learning from a very young age (Gross, 1999).

Do you understand the abilities that every child in your classroom has? Make sure you are not focused on the disability or what is missing. Find the child's strength and work with that!

Teacher Tips!

◆ Use collaborative projects that provide a meaningful role for each learner.
◆ Pay close attention to the level of challenge provided for each child. Sometimes challenging behaviors reveal that a child is facing too much or too little challenge in their school activities.

- ◆ Be prepared to relinquish some control of classroom time. For young children to engage in active learning at their own developmental level, they must have plenty of time to explore, discuss, and experience actions and materials with less guidance from the teacher.
- ◆ Teachers should focus on highlighting key vocabulary and concepts for each child by using developmentally responsive scaffolding techniques.
- ◆ Resist the culture of learned helplessness—let them do it!
- ◆ Be very aware of classroom aides or special education aides who over support children because they think that is their job. All of your jobs are to make the child as independent as possible so they can learn and be part of the classroom and community.
- ◆ Have open-ended materials that are flexible enough that all students can learn from them. If the object only has one purpose and one way to do something, look for another object instead.
- ◆ Find materials that you can use to make classroom materials easier to use and manipulate. Materials such as modeling clay, sponge hair curlers, rubber bands, tennis balls, ace bandages, cardboard, foam board, and different types of tape can make handles bigger, sturdier, and even easier for some students to grip. Even paper clips put on pages of a book can make it easier for children to turn the pages individually.

DECAL: Active Learning for Children from Different Languages
Even though children may not be fluent in the language of
the classroom, instruction in content and skills must go on.
Teachers need to supplement their instruction with some
use of the child's native language as well as many alternative
communication strategies. The most important thing is to try
to ensure that the child understands and is understood. This
is important as they develop friendship with peers who do
not speak the language, and it is important for the teacher to
be able to assess what the child knows and can do.

Can every person in your classroom communicate with
each other? Are there ways for everyone to talk and for
everyone to understand what is being said to them?

Teacher Tips!

◆ Remind parents that being bilingual is
a wonderful thing, and encourage the
continued use of the native language at home.
Assure the parents that this will not hurt the
child academically in any way— and, in fact,
it may help in the long run.

◆ Pair all instruction with concrete materials that
the children can see, touch, and manipulate to
bring meaning to the words in English.

◆ Use non-verbal cues such as gestures,
and teach the child to use them, too, to
communicate with you and with their peers.

◆ In addition to gestures, work on a way that
children who speak different languages can
communicate and interact with each other
during play in the classroom. PECS, which has

primarily been used for children who have a speech and language disability, comes in handy when two children speak different languages.

◆ Create a common classroom language using pictures and words written in both languages so children can use them to talk to each other.

◆ Give the child some time to process language. Classrooms can seem very overwhelming and demanding when the child is learning a second language. Give them some space to process it all.

◆ Learning to understand the concepts and content in the child's home language is much more important that learning to speak English (Espinosa, 2013).

◆ Supporting active learning and communication rather than the passive learning of isolated words and skills will help those young brains develop as they should, whether in one language or two or more languages (Nemeth, 2012).

◆ Use concrete items and take time to explain and demonstrate the meanings of words for all children, helping children who speak different languages make connections between new words and words they already know in the home language (Ackerman & Tazi, 2015).

Multiple Means of Action and Expression—Routines and Schedules

Routines and schedules are an important learning tool within a developmentally appropriate early childhood classroom. Predictable routines in the classroom help children to feel safe and secure since they know what to expect during the day. When classrooms stick to a familiar schedule, children are more likely to master the routines of the day, like cleaning up the centers and getting ready for lunch.

DECAL: Routines and Schedules for Children from Different Experiences

Instability with routines in early childhood can impact many parts of a child's development. Frequent and prolonged instability can cause young children to feel a significant amount of stress, which will negatively impact early academics and social/emotional skills.

Teacher Tips!

- Children with unstable home lives may crave the routines of the classroom and may have a difficult time when the routine is changed. Make sure you prepare them well in advance and often, so there are no problems.
- Children with unstable home lives crave autonomy and may not respond well to adults dictating what they can and cannot do. Make sure you give children with these needs choices within the classroom.
- A key influence on school readiness is preschool attendance; if children are not coming to school regularly, have your school administration work with the parents to understand the importance and help overcome some of the barriers (Isaacs, 2012).

DECAL: Routines and Schedules for Children from Different Cultures

Certain cultures and groups view time in a linear fashion, doing only one thing at a time and within a fixed schedule; other cultures view time in a less linear way. Some cultures are less focused on schedules or punctuality.

Teacher Tips!

◆ Instead of blaming the children for being late to school or having a hard time following the classroom schedule, consider these behaviors may be culturally driven, so alternatives need to be developed.

[handwritten note: School attendance]

DECAL: Routines and Schedules for Children with Different Abilities

Providing children with disabilities the opportunities to learn within the regular routines of the general education classroom is essential. Removing children with disabilities from the routines and activities of the general education classroom in order to provide related services at a time that accommodates the schedule of adults is disruptive and promotes the generalization of skills within the natural environment (McWilliam & Scott, 2001).

Teacher Tips!

◆ Work with therapists to embed therapies within the classroom so the classroom teacher can learn from observing and contributing to the therapeutic interventions.

(continued)

> *(continued)*
>
> ◆ Work to provide extra activities in the classroom, so the child has more opportunities to practice the new therapeutic techniques.

DECAL: Routines and Schedules for Children from Different Languages

As with children from different cultures, the explanation of some routines and schedules may not make sense to some children who speak different languages.

Teacher Tips!

◆ Teach the meanings of words and phrases about time in a more concrete manner. Avoid using vague terms like "later" that have no specific meaning.
◆ Use images to depict the events in the daily schedule.

Multiple Means of Action and Expression—Ongoing Assessment

Ongoing assessment helps teachers and the school make better decisions for children. The more we know about what children know and can do independently, the better we can design developmentally appropriate activities and programs for them.

DECAL: Ongoing Assessment for Children from Different Experiences

Children who have different experiences are difficult to assess. It is essential that teachers understand the difference between a lack of exposure to specific content and skills vs. a difficulty with learning specific content and skills.

Teacher Tips!

- The earlier the intervention the better. Research has proven that high-quality preschool has potential life-long benefits (Magnuson, 2013).
- Catch specific skills, like the specific precursors to reading skills, as early as you can. New research looks at reading skills down to the earliest years of childhood, broadening our understanding of the early factors that are associated with success and failure in reading (Annie E. Casey Foundation, 2013a).

DECAL: Ongoing Assessment for Children from Different Cultures

Many early childhood assessments were not developed for students from different cultures, and because they do not consider cultural difference, they may not be assessing what we think they are assessing. Standardized assessments will not be accurate for children from different cultures.

The NAEYC and the National Association of Early Childhood Specialists in State Departments of Education (NAECS/SDE) published a position statement on early childhood curriculum, assessment, and program evaluation (NAEYC, NAECS/SDE, 2003). In this position statement, the key assessment recommendation is to assess young children's strengths, progress, and needs, using assessment methods that are developmentally appropriate, culturally and linguistically responsive, tied to children's daily activities, supported by professional development, inclusive of families, and connected to specific, beneficial purposes, including

- ◆ assessment that it used to make sound decisions about teaching and learning,
- ◆ assessment that is used to identify significant concerns that may require focused intervention,
- ◆ assessment that is used to help programs improve their educational and developmental interventions.

(NAECS/SDE, p. 24–25)

Teacher Tips!

- ◆ Assess children from different cultures in the natural environment and across many different opportunities.
- ◆ Talk to people who know what the cultural expectations are before you use assessments to make decisions.

DECAL: Ongoing Assessment for Children with Different Abilities

For young children with disabilities, assessments are always individualized and are used to determine services and guide instruction, as well as develop the accommodations and supports that may be necessary.

Teacher Tips!

- ◆ Each child's progress is measured in the context of their own prior knowledge, not measured against other children.
- ◆ Assessments need to reflect what the child can do independently and with assistance, and the two levels need to be addressed.

DECAL: Ongoing Assessment for Children from Different Languages

For students who are not fluent in English, as with students from different cultures, any standardized assessment should be looked at with caution.

Teacher Tips!

- ◆ For informal classroom assessments, assess students using their preferred language as much as possible.
- ◆ For formal evaluations, higher stakes assessments must be based on multiple methods and measures featuring age-appropriate and culturally and linguistically appropriate tools. To have a more comprehensive look at the child, the assessments should be ongoing and involve two or more adults, repeating assessments of language development over time (NAEYC, 2009).

Multiple Means of Action and Expression—Teacher Resources

Teacher Self-Assessment Questions

◆ Am I sure that every child has the basic instruction in how to use items in the classroom that they have never had access to before? Is it that they do not know how to cut paper with scissors or have they never had the opportunity to have scissors in their own hands before?

◆ Am I sure that every child knows what the pretend play props in my classroom are and what they are used for? They may not have context of how some of the props in the classroom are used.

◆ Reflect on your own culture and teaching style to see how it may differ from the students you are teaching, and how teachers working from their own cultures and teaching styles can successfully reach the diverse populations in most schools today.

◆ Ask yourself, do I understand the cultural expectations for participation from a child from this culture? Should boys and girls participate in the same group as peers or culturally, would it be expected that they be separated? How can I change my way of doing things to fit what they would be comfortable doing?

◆ How will children of different cultures best demonstrate what they know? Would letting them get up in front of the whole class be a good thing or frowned upon culturally?

◆ Have you made it easy for children with different needs to physically complete the activity and participate with peers without adult assistance?

◆ How do you get a child who may not be as independent as the others to participate and demonstrate what they know and can do? How do you support and help the child without over-helping them and doing it for them? How do you make sure the child is learning to be independent and not dependent on adults?

◆ How are you challenging students who are gifted or may be advanced in particular areas in order to give them the opportunity to explore further while still making sure they are part of the group?

◆ Is every child's home language represented in some way in some place in the classroom?

◆ What have you done to learn key words and phrases of the languages the children in your classroom speak?

◆ What have you done to teach (or have someone else come in and teach) all the students in the classroom words and phrases in the languages of all the children in the classroom?

◆ How have you achieved a balance between supporting the home languages and facilitating the learning of English? Being bilingual is an asset, and all teachers should encourage the child and the family to become fluent in the family's native language, even if it is a language that the teacher does not know.

4

Using UDL as a Framework

Providing Multiple Means of Engagement

What Does This Mean to a Teacher?

Being engaged means more than just being on task; it means the child has a desire to know more, to do more, and to be part of more. When we talk about multiple means of engagement, we are looking at children's interest as well as their behavior in the classroom. Children who are engaged show signs that they are curious and want to know more about how the world works. When children are engaged and intrinsically motivated, they are more likely to be able to persist through difficulties and setbacks.

Guided Questions

- ◆ How much time do children spend together in play?
- ◆ Do you have times of the day when children must work alone or work in groups? How much flexibility do you offer with that?

◆ How much of your instruction relies on rote learning of concepts such as letters, numbers, colors, and shapes? How much of your instruction is about teaching specific routines that all children must follow? Are there any times when children can figure things out all on their own?

◆ When you step back and just watch, what materials do children show the most interest in? Do you have a way you want children to play or use those materials? Do children have time in the day to explore with those materials any way they want?

Multiple Means of Engagement

Children learn through play. Experimenting with different materials and playing with different peers helps children build new knowledge based on what they already know and can do. The choices teachers make with how they plan the day and how the room and different materials are arranged helps make learning more concrete for children.

Different children need different amounts of time to support the learning that works best for them. To be responsive to the needs of all children, a schedule with some flexibility will work best. Some teachers provide options for children who can't sustain attention to an activity as long as others. So, there might be related independent play options such as table toys related to the scheduled activity, or books. It is important, however, that these options should not be simple "busy work," and they should be planned to represent content that will support connections to what other children are learning at the same time. Plenty of time should be allowed for children who work at a slower pace.

On the other hand, this time allowance should not leave the quicker children with nothing to do. When preparing for transitions, for example, some children will be ready to end their activity and line up quickly. Others need more time. The children who were first to line up shouldn't suffer for their choice by having to stand idly while some other children gradually finish up and get ready to transition. The teacher could plan transition activities such as discussion questions or learning songs that would engage the children who are ready early and help all children learn to be patient with those who work at a different pace. Ideally, each part of the daily schedule should be more like a menu of options than an exact time frame with exact requirements.

DECAL: Engagement for Children from Different Experiences

Teachers need to understand the different experiences a child has had interacting with materials (i.e., computers, pretend play toys) from other children in the classroom. Some children may not have had many experiences with some materials in the classroom, so pretending with them may not come naturally.

> What open-ended and novel materials can you add to the classroom for children to engage with? What rules will you have about these materials, and do you think those rules will impact how the child engages?

Teacher Tips!

- ◆ For children who have fears about using open-ended materials "incorrectly," start small and work toward positive open-ended imaginative play. Model it for them.

(continued)

(continued)

- ◆ Have minimal basic rules for children who crave the structure. The rules can be as simple as how many students can be with the materials at one time and where the materials can be played with.
- ◆ Children who have lived in poverty or who are homeless may have difficulty sharing materials that they have started to engage with. Respect those experiences and give them their own set of the materials that they can store safely, so they can count on them being there.
- ◆ Some children will be ritualistic in their play, so adding novel materials that are at the top of the zone of proximal development and are used with assistance may break some habits.

DECAL: Engagement for Children from Different Cultures

Culture is more than just an ethnic label; it can also impact how children interact and engage with others. Some cultures value being independent and some cultures value working together as a group, and that is important to understand in the classroom. These cultural expectations can come through in the class with the choices of who to play with, when, and the roles children take within the classroom (Kaiser & Rasminsky, 2016).

How deep is my knowledge and how wide are my experiences with the cultures of the children in my class? Do I have any "blind spots" when it comes to understanding how their culture changes the way they engage in the classroom?

Teacher Tips!

◆ Don't try to change the children's cultural expectations and values. Work on developing each child's identity and find value in each other's culture.

◆ Change your own expectations of engagement in the classroom, be comfortable with the differences of children from different cultures, and do not promote what your own culture values.

◆ Be flexible, offer opportunities to work on long-term projects together while also carving out time for some students to work on their own. Project-based learning is very successful in the universally designed classroom.

DECAL: Engagement for Children with Different Abilities

It is important to understand how the child's abilities and disabilities impact engagement. Intellectual delays and disabilities will inhibit maturity, making engagement with peers and materials in the classroom with typically developing peers more difficult (but never impossible).

Do children's individual delays and disabilities make it harder for them to engage with peers, or engage in classroom routines or activities?

Teacher Tips!

- ◆ Look at how the materials are used by the children in the class. Can all of the children use them in the way they are meant to be used, or do you have to adapt them?
- ◆ Look at the routine of the child with a disability. Do they have enough time to engage with their peers in play, or are they sometimes out for a therapy of some kind, or working with a teacher or aide on a specific skill. Watch that you are sacrificing time for them to engage with peers.

DECAL: Engagement for Children from Different Languages

When young children want to communicate with peers, their common language is not always verbal. The use of sign language, gestures, and pictures to facilitate interaction and engagement with classmates and friends can be successful. Don't let language differences be a barrier to engagement. Large group activities, which encourage children to help each other without language, assist them to learn the value of each other's friendship across the language barrier (Nemeth, 2011).

Do you make a conscious effort to make sure that all children, no matter what their language of preference, have a way to communicate with each other?

Teacher Tips!

- ◆ Have the teachers model learning a classmate's unfamiliar language. The teachers can use gestures and pictures, too!
- ◆ Allow children time to just play with their friends, watching how children try to communicate on their own, and help support that.
- ◆ Make sure you work with *all* the parents to have them help support *all* the languages in the classroom.

Having the time and the right materials to promote engagement is one of the important things teachers can do in the classroom. Facilitating engagement works on important skills children need both now and for the rest of their lives, like curiosity and persistence. When children are truly engaged, they are naturally curious and are inclined to explore and ask questions. When children are truly engaged, they can persist through tasks and be attentive to the smallest details. Help children learn to help each other rather than always relying on an adult. Every empowered child has something to offer a friend. Engagement can seem loud sometimes and can look unstructured, but it is valuable. Engagement is an important aspect of any classroom to promote lifelong skills.

5

Where We Are Now and Where We Need to Go

Sometimes the status quo is the biggest obstacle to change. That concept is especially true when we discuss what we do in schools today. For many years, children have been grouped into silos by what is the "same." Classrooms become silos made up of children who are the same age and children who live in the same neighborhood, but in reality, children are not all the same. Some children have differing abilities, or come from different places, speak different languages, and have had different experiences. We know that not everyone fits into the same silo.

Guided Questions

◆ How has your program changed over the last five years? How about the past 10 or 15 years?
◆ What is the most challenging part of serving the needs of all the children in your program?

◆ What barriers have you already faced and what
barriers do you expect to face in the near future?
◆ What new knowledge do you think the
professionals in your program need? What new
knowledge do you think you need?

All Together Now—The New Normal

Classroom practices have changed over the years.
Academics and direct instruction have become carefully
controlled, with the teacher defining what content and
skills the children are supposed to learn and when they
need to learn it. The whole concept of "school-readiness
skills" has young children learning pre-academic work at
younger and younger ages. All of this "drill and kill" of
specific and isolated knowledge, referred to as "work" in
some preschool classes, is expressly different to children
than is "play," and all this work is giving children less
time to learn the most important skill—how to learn.

Early childhood classrooms of today are also more
inclusive than they have ever been before. Children are
coming to our classrooms with different life and familial
experiences. They are coming from families from different
cultures than our own. They have different abilities and disabilities. Their native language may be different from the
group, or they may have more than one of these differences
at the same time. While we say diversity should be cele-
brated, teachers are facing more and more pressure from
standardized expectations, and we may be unintentionally
exacerbating the challenges they face in the classroom.

So who are the children in our classrooms today?

Children from Different Experiences

Poverty

As of 2013, 51% of children in public schools qualify for free or subsidized school meals, with 22% of children living below the official poverty line (Annie E. Casey Foundation, 2013b). The issue of poverty is also concentrated in certain groups. In 2013, nearly 40% of all African American children lived below the poverty line. The poverty rate for other groups is not as severe, but it is worrisome, with 37% of Native American children and 33% of Hispanic children living in poverty. These children are more than twice as likely to live in poverty compared to Caucasian children, with only 14% of Caucasian children living below the poverty line.

Neighborhoods

Even if children do not live in poverty themselves, just living in a community where over 30% of the community is in poverty will have an impact on them. Where there is a concentration of poverty, schools tend to be lower performing, local employment is harder to come by, and violence and crime are more prevalent. According to the research by the Annie E. Casey Foundation (2013b), 14% of children were living in neighborhoods with a high level of concentrated poverty, which is up from 9% from 2000. According to the report, almost one third of African American children and 30% of Latino children live in areas of concentrated poverty.

Family Structure

Family structures are increasingly varied. What may have been a typical family when teachers and administrators were growing up may be less common now. According to a Pew Research Center report in 2013, only 46% of children are living with two married heterosexual parents who are in their first marriage, which is down from 61% in 1980 and 73% in 1960 (Livingston, 2014). The data also show that the institution of marriage itself is changing, with more than 41% of children being born outside a traditional marriage, up from only 5% in 1960. One of the most significant changes in this data shows that 34% of children are living with one unmarried parent, which is up from 19% in 1980 and just 9% in 1960 (Livingston, 2014).

Children may live with their grandparents, or guardians, or multiple parents, or same-sex parents or internationally adoptive parents, and their family structure may change more often than families changed in the past. The structure of families presented in the 1950s sitcoms is no longer relevant for today.

What Teachers Need to Know

- ◆ Everyone is unique and everyone has strengths. Build resiliency in children by building up what they can do and empower them to focus on what is good.
- ◆ Check your experience at the door; remember that how you grew up or live now may be different from the children in your class. Respect that their families are making the best decisions possible based on their reality.
- ◆ Keep your expectations high; all children will strive to meet those expectations.
- ◆ Include families in the classroom as much as you can. Everyone can contribute and be included.

- ◆ Become a mentor, either officially or unofficially. Most of the people who made it out of the poverty they grew up in did it with the help of a mentor.
- ◆ Families come in all configurations, but focus on whom the children consider their family. It may include more people or different people than you are prepared for.

Children from Different Cultures

US Government data from 2015 indicates that there are more than 61 million legal and illegal immigrants in this country with children under the age of 18, with at least 75% of those children from parents who immigrated here legally (Ziegler & Camarota, 2016). This group of Americans is relatively new and is growing at a quick pace, with a growth rate six times faster than the total population between 1970 and 2015. Illegal immigration has also changed American schools, with a 2015 estimate of around 5.1 million school-aged children living in this county with a parent who is an illegal immigrant.

The United States has always been a multicultural society, but what was once the *melting pot*—when families left their cultural traditions behind in order to assimilate into the "American" culture, we are now more of a *salad bowl*, where many different cultures can exist together side by side and never lose their uniqueness.

When we talk about culture, we are more commonly speaking of values, norms, traditions, and conformity. When we talk about young children from different cultures it is particularly important to understand specific aspects of their culture. For young children, play reflects what is meaningful to them within their own lives. Cultural, social, and familial values and practices tend to shape how children play (Erickson, 1963; Vygotsky, 1977).

What Teachers Need to Know

- ◆ Young children learn many of their own societal roles, norms, and values through play.
- ◆ Children from European American cultures tend to focus on independence and how children can do things for themselves.
- ◆ Children from Asian, African, or Hispanic American cultures may focus on social-emotional factors and how children act as a member of a group.
- ◆ Families of young children from Asian cultures see play and academics as two different things, with academics more highly valued of the two, whereas families of young children from some European cultures see little difference between play and academic learning.

Children with Different Abilities and Disabilities

Most children develop and grow at their own pace, but the stages or pattern of development are usually very similar. Some children develop advanced gross motor skills while their speech and language skills may lag. Eventually most children develop the skills they need to support their own interests and activities. Some children are born with disabilities or acquire disabilities that have them develop outside the norm, and researchers classify these disabilities as either physical, neurodevelopmental/ mental health, or other.

Children with Disabilities

The number of children who are diagnosed with a disability is about 6 million, which is approximately 16% of the population, and the number is on the rise. Research finds that the rate of children who are diagnosed with a disability has increased by 16.3% in just a decade (Houtrow, Kandyce-Larson, Olson, & Newacheck, 2014). The kinds of disabilities, and who is being diagnosed, have varied. The number of physical disabilities has decreased in the past decade, but the number of young children, specifically young children who come from affluent backgrounds, is increasing with both neurodevelopmental and mental health-related disabilities. Most notably is that the trend for children under the age of 6 to be diagnosed with a neurodevelopmental disability has doubled from 19 cases per 1,000 children to 36 cases per 1,000 children (Houtrow et al., 2014). Neurodevelopmental disabilities include ADHD, learning disabilities, and autism.

Children Who Are Gifted

Young children can also develop at a pace much quicker than their peers can. Developmentally, gifted children generally tend to develop speech, motor skills, and social/emotional skills earlier than their peers do (Karnes, Manning, Besnoy, Cukierkorn, & Houston, 2005). Some types of giftedness, such as artistically gifted or musically gifted, are not usually found in young children since those skills require a significant amount of time to cultivate those skills. It is important to know that gifted preschoolers are likely to initiate their own learning and demonstrate high levels of curiosity about how things work (Karnes et al., 2005).

Early Diagnosis and Intervention

Early diagnosis and intervention are probably the most important things a teacher can do to help a child with a disability or a potential disability. Many parents, teachers, and doctors take a "wait and see" approach that can ultimately delay getting the child the early help they need. New research from the Center for Disease Control and Prevention Autism and Developmental Disabilities Monitoring Network (2016) reported that only 43% of young children with autism had received an evaluation by the time they were 3 years old, even though 87% of those children showed signs of of Autism well before the age of 3.

Early intervention is also important for young children who are gifted in order to prevent underachievement (Stile, Kitano, Kelley, & LeCrone, 1993). A rich and stimulating environment with novel materials and time for them to explore on their own is important to enhance their high levels of curiosity. Classrooms need to prepare the environment and change their daily practices to let children who are gifted develop their own pattern for learning.

What Teachers Need to Know

- ◆ It is okay for every child to have their own rate of development. Keep track of each child as an individual and help them achieve at their own pace.
- ◆ Not everything has to be the same for every child. The classroom can have different materials that are specifically for different children, including some for children who are developing more slowly and for those who are developing quickly.
- ◆ Ask for help if you need help, or, if you suspect that the child may have a disability or the child may be gifted, ask. Most of the time your instincts are correct.

Children Who Speak Different Languages

As of 2013, nearly one in three children in the U.S. lived in a household where more than one language is spoken (Child Trends Databank, 2014). This trend is on the rise, increasing from 20 million children to 23 million children between 2004 and 2013, an increase from 28% to 32%, with 23% of those children speaking Spanish as their primary language.

Learning a new language takes time, especially for young children who are continuing to learn their home language. Research tells us that it can take between four and seven years for a young child to become proficient enough in English for academic purposes (Center for Public Education, 2007). Becoming proficient in English that is used for academics by the end of first grade is important, since research tells us that students who are proficient in the English used in classrooms by the end of the first grade have better outcomes that those children who are not (Halle, Hair, McNamara, Wandner, & Chien, 2012). But becoming proficient in English at the determent of the home language is not the answer.

Years of research tell us that having the child continue to use and learn their home language is not just good but essential. The research and the mandates are clear; children must be supported in learning their home language. This is reflected in policy and position statements from the Office of Head Start (2007), NAEYC (2005), DEC (2010), Office of English Language Acquisition (Pinkos, 2007), National Literacy Panel (August & Shanahan, 2008), the National Task Force on Early Childhood Education for Hispanics (2007), and from researchers including Patton Tabors (2008) and Linda Espinosa (2013).

What Teachers Need to Know

- ◆ It is very important to have all the languages of all the children evident in the classroom, and to have books, games, posters, and labels in the home language displayed throughout the classroom (with pronunciations if needed).
- ◆ You need to learn some words and phrases of each of the home languages of children in your classroom. Ask the parents—and the children—to teach you!
- ◆ Thread your activities and learning for a few days at a time so young dual language learners can make connections and use new vocabulary in context (Nemeth, 2009).

Why Is UDL, and Especially DECAL, so Important?

UDL has been used effectively for many years to help teachers plan for the needs for students with disabilities in their classrooms, but just using UDL for individuals with disabilities is no longer enough. When we proactively design the way we teach, the materials we use, and how we assess ALL students in many different ways, everyone can succeed (Ralabate, 2011).

We need to have a revolution, at least a little one, and break some of these silos down. We know that schools in the past (and maybe some still today) were standardized, teaching the same thing to every student, and rewarding those students who complied with the rules. Teachers expected students to repeat isolated knowledge back to them, to behave properly, to complete tasks on command, and to respond when requested. The workforce of the future will require diverse workers prepared to work collaboratively with diverse co-workers. Children, especially young children, should be learning to solve real problems and learning to ask real questions instead of memorizing and repeating facts, and that is where our old practices need to change. Inclusive classrooms and inclusive lives will be normal. A whole host of languages and new and emerging cultures will be part of the every-day landscape. We must prepare students for things we ourselves do not even understand, jobs we have never heard of before, and communities that are fully inclusive. We must teach the next generation of professionals to think through the lens of DECAL.

6

Professional Development Resources

Using the UDL Framework Across the DECAL— Elements to Support Change in Professional Practices

What Does This Mean to a Teacher?

Teachers often experience professional development as a series of separate topic-focused workshops. If you attend a math workshop, you probably did not get specific information about adapting the materials for children with limited dexterity. If you take an assistive technology workshop, you probably did not get information about how to use the strategies with children who speak different languages. Teacher training often happens in silos that make it hard for you to put together the various recommendations and requirements being presented to you. When you can be an active participant in professional development that presents clear implementation goals and responds to individual adult learning needs, you take on ownership of your professional learning. The UDL framework not only changes how teachers teach, it can also improve how teachers learn. This perspective places a greater share of professional development responsibility on you as an adult learner. We will show you how this works in the context of UDL. This chapter is intended to empower educators as adult learners and to inform professional development providers about these methods. We firmly believe that early childhood education is not just a job—it's a profession. Professions are not determined by salary. They are determined by dedication to excellence and to constantly learning and building one's knowledge and skills.

Guided Questions

- ◆ What is the best professional development experience you've had? Can you describe what makes it so memorable?
- ◆ How does your school help you learn from and with your peers?
- ◆ What is your administrator's role in professional development?

How Did We Get Where We Are Today?

Separate Preparation Systems

The way we train our educator workforce is antiquated, and everyone needs to have more than just a basic understanding of the needs of all children (Mulvey, Cooper, Accurso, & Garliardi, 2014). Just knowing the basics of how to teach is not enough. Teachers must now know about how to have high-quality interactions with children and how to prevent challenging and explosive behaviors for all children. The skills for individualizing instruction and scaffolding learning, both proactively and reactively, are essential to twenty-first-century educators and beyond.

Preparation for teaching different categories of children remains segregated in higher education programs by licensure requirements. We can reform notions of teacher success when we realize that teachers teach in their silos because they were taught to teach in our silos. We are seeing promising results in colleges where departments for early childhood education, special education, and English as a second language collaborate to create a more seamless system of teacher preparation.

Separate Pre-K and K Systems

Advancements have been made in linking pre-K systems to the state K–12 systems in the United States, but unfortunately, unstable state funding has limited this growth. According to the 2015 *State of Preschool* report from the National Center for Early Education Research (2016), approximately 1.4 million children attended a K–12-linked, state-funded pre-K in 2015, serving just 20% of 4-year-olds and just 5% of 3-year-olds. Other public programs, including non-state-funded public preschool and federally funded special education programs and Head Start, serve approximately 41% of 4-year-olds and 16% of 3-year-olds, so where are more than half the children who are preschool age? Where are they spending their days?

Even though most school districts serve preschoolers in some way, there is often a disconnect between the preschool services and the K–12 services. Federal guidance and ESSA requirements seek to change this condition by encouraging a more seamless approach that includes shared professional development and intentional planning. UDL could be an effective approach that supports this connection.

Silos of Philosophy

The philosophies between some preschools and the K–3 system can differ. Early childhood philosophy and curriculum used in preschool classrooms are holistic, looking at the development of the child as a whole, not just as a reader or writer. High-quality early childhood curriculum is grounded in child development theory and years of research. K–3 systems are usually bound by the K–12 model, and starting this change in Kindergarten is a problem.

In their report, *Crisis in Kindergarten*, authors Miller and Almon (2009) reported that teaching to the state standards and increasing student achievement on standardized assessments of isolated skills have become the central focus for many classrooms and programs. This new focus is leading administrators and some teachers to embrace highly scripted programs that do not support child-directed play and offer little time for exploration and imagination.

Silos of Practice

While pre-K is most likely in its own silo away from K, even within preschool we have our own silos. Young children with disabilities are still being segregated and taught with other children with disabilities. Many times, specialists in special education and speech therapy pull young children away from their peers to practice isolated skills of the adults' choosing. Young children who are dual language learners are often segregated within classrooms where they work with a classroom aide who is the only adult speaking the same language. With all this segregated knowledge, segregated philosophy, and segregated practices, it is no wonder the status quo never changes.

How Do We Change? New Perspectives on Professional Development

Adults approach professional learning based on their own different experiences, cultures, abilities, and languages—an adult version of DECAL. Understanding the UDL framework through the DECAL lens can be used to help programs, presenters, and teachers re-imagine professional development to achieve greater benefits and observable outcomes by focusing on the individual needs of adult learners. The key difference is in setting goals. Instead of setting a goal to arrange a speaker on a particular topic, the goal should address what needs to be learned with a plan for a variety of ways to learn it based on individual and group needs. The focus should be on making the new information accessible to each individual who needs it and on looking for evidence that change has happened as a result of that learning. Too often, current efforts focus on checking off that everyone has attended a workshop without questioning what participants gained and what each participant will do as a result of their attendance. When you change the goal to focus on changing practice with new skills and information, you open the door to a more universal approach to providing that information.

The UDL framework applied to adult learning connects very strongly to the principles of adult learning that were pioneered by Malcolm Knowles (Knowles, Holton, & Swanson, 2015). Knowles has made the case that each adult learns in unique ways because of their lifetime of developing preferences, prior knowledge, and experiences. As mature thinkers, adults are especially able to benefit from seeing the long-term applicability of what they are learning, and they are especially likely to be frustrated when that long-term applicability is not clear to them. Here are the principles of effective adult learning that are attributed to Knowles (Knowles et al., 2015):

1. Adults need to understand why they need to learn new information.
2. Adults need to see themselves as effective, self-directed learners.
3. Adults will experience new learning through the lens of their prior knowledge and experiences.
4. Adults need environments and experiences that make them feel ready to learn.
5. Adults learn best when the new knowledge is focused on solving a problem they need to solve.
6. Adult learning is especially affected by the individual's level of motivation and belief that the new knowledge will be useful to them.

For early childhood educators, these principles can be seen as the adult version of DAP. They give you important insights into how you can benefit from taking responsibility for your own professional learning by working with professional development providers. Those providers can help you learn what you need to know by addressing you as an individual, considering where you are along the learning continuum based on your own experiences and culture, and by supporting your individual motivations and interests, just as you do when working with young children.

According to the *Early Childhood Education Professional Development, Training and Technical Assistance Glossary* developed by NAEYC and NACCRRA (2011, p. 5):

All professional development (education, training, and TA) should

- be designed using evidence-based best practices; consistent with the principles of adult learning; and structured to promote linkages between research, theory, and practice;
- address the continuum of young children's abilities and needs;
- respond to each learner's background (including cultural, linguistic, and ability), experiences, and the current context of her role and professional goals;
- include resources to ensure access for all.

Now let's see how the elements of the UDL framework can help make professional development more effective for all.

UDL—Representation

Professional development materials can be presented for listening, reading, or hands-on experiences. Information and skills can be conveyed to adult audiences in any of these ways:

- Spoken presentations
- Distance learning via webinar, MOOC, or online course that allows interaction
- Print on paper books, articles, or handouts
- Digital print in ebooks and apps
- Combinations of images and print via PowerPoint or similar
- Recorded video
- Recorded audio
- Still photograph
- Charts, tables, and other images

- ◆ Animation
- ◆ Infographics
- ◆ Hands-on demonstrations
- ◆ Social media posts and comments
- ◆ Site visits.

There are many different media tools to convey information that early childhood educators might need or want to learn. Recognizing the formats that work best for you will help you plan for your own professional learning successfully. Professional development leaders can use the DECAL system to consider how these different media can be made more accessible to individual learners.

Guidance for Professional Development Providers

DECAL: Professional Development Materials and Media to Meet the Needs of Adult Learners from Different Experiences

Prior experience with different media will influence how adults respond to professional development. Some people have had a lot of experience reading charts and tables, but others find them confusing. People who are comfortable with technology tools may be better able to access ebooks or digital information. Some reflection will be needed to clarify what will work for individuals and groups of participants. The UDL approach places the focus on proactively adapting the learning materials and environment to provide multiple pathways for learning rather than waiting to make reactive adaptations to individual participants. The focus for adaptation should be placed on making the environment ready for diverse participants rather than on the individual participant trying to adapt to challenging environments (Rose, Harbour, Johnston, Daley, & Abarbanell, 2006).

Professional Development Tips!

- ◆ Print should be large enough and clear enough, on screens and on paper, to accommodate those with vision challenges.
- ◆ Print should also be provided at a vocabulary and literacy level that makes the information accessible to all intended audiences.
- ◆ Printed information should be translated so that each adult learner can experience the depth of understanding by reading in their home language.
- ◆ Video examples should be accompanied by transcripts for people who may find it hard to follow the visual or auditory tracks.
- ◆ Professional development settings should be free from distracting noise and discomfort.
- ◆ Images should be meaningful enough to support understanding—not just entertaining.
- ◆ Professional development materials and information should be available to all who need them without cost barriers.
- ◆ Real materials promote learning better than pictures, and hands-on practice builds learning better than passively listening to instructions.

DECAL: Professional Development Materials and Media to Meet the Needs of Adult Learners from Different Cultures

Images and speaking styles have cultural components, too. Keep in mind that information is more readily learned when it is presented in ways that are familiar to the learners.

Professional Development Tips!

- ◆ Be sure the characters and people in the material are representative of the diverse ethnicities, cultures, and lifestyles of your program.
- ◆ Be sure that the print and spoken words are not offensive to any culture.

DECAL: Professional Development Materials and Media to Meet the Needs of Adult Learners with Different Abilities

Technology can help adult learners with different abilities to find ways to receive information that meets their needs. Technology can also make it possible for adult learners with different abilities to find a way to express what they are learning that is comfortable for them. Here are some adaptations that may help.

Professional Development Tips!

- ◆ Print should be large enough to accommodate those with vision challenges.
- ◆ Print should also be provided at a vocabulary and literacy level that makes the information accessible to all audiences.
- ◆ Video examples should be accompanied by transcripts for people who may find it hard to follow the visual or auditory tracks.
- ◆ Simple fonts make reading easier.
- ◆ Professional development settings should be free from distracting noise and discomfort.
- ◆ Some adult learners may need to receive information in smaller chunks with frequent breaks.

- Some adult learners benefit from learning key information via verbal explanation in addition to written materials.

DECAL: Professional Development Materials and Media to Meet the Needs of Adult Learners from Different Languages

When an early childhood educator speaks a language other than English, that additional language can be an important asset in the program. Providing materials in the languages spoken by the adults in your program helps them to gain important depth of understanding and helps them to continue to grow and develop their non-English language.

Professional Development Tips!

- Print should be translated when possible.
- Video and audio materials should have transcripts that can be translated.
- Images that are associated with print information can help bilingual adults make learning connections.
- Some websites provide professional learning materials for early childhood educators in more than one language. Look for Colorín Colorado (www.colorincolorado.org) and the Early Childhood Learning & Knowledge Center (www.eclkc.ohs.acf.hhs.gov/hslc/tta-system).
- The Google Translate app for mobile devices allows the user to use his camera to scan print and show it on the screen in translated form.

UDL—Action/Expression

As we explore the role of the adult learner in determining her own professional learning, the UDL principle of addressing multiple means of action and expression plays a critical role. As we described in Chapter 3, we think of action as the mental action or learning activity undertaken by the learner, and we think of expression as addressing multiple ways for the learner to show what they have learned. These principles are just as relevant to adult learners as they are to children, and they encourage an approach that responds to each individual learner. Here are some ways that an adult learner might engage in professional learning:

- ◆ Viewing live presentations
- ◆ Participating in distance learning via webinar, MOOC, or online courses that allow interaction
- ◆ Reading print on paper books, articles, or handouts
- ◆ Reading digital print in ebooks, websites, and apps
- ◆ Reading combinations of images and print via PowerPoint-type presentations or infographics
- ◆ Viewing recorded video clips or full-length documentaries
- ◆ Listening to recorded audio books or podcasts
- ◆ Studying still photographs
- ◆ A book study group
- ◆ Formalized lesson studies or other professional learning communities
- ◆ Reviewing charts, tables, and other images
- ◆ Viewing animation videos
- ◆ Participating in hands-on demonstrations

- ◆ Consulting, coaching, and mentoring interactions
- ◆ Acting in role-playing demonstrations
- ◆ Learning via game format
- ◆ Studying with self-guided learning programs
- ◆ Filling in worksheets
- ◆ Reading social media posts and comments
- ◆ Receiving email newsletters and list servs
- ◆ Learning via informal conversations
- ◆ Attending workshops
- ◆ Seeking out conference presentations
- ◆ Becoming inspired by keynote speeches.

Keep in mind that in order to be most effective, each teacher, administrator, specialist, and paraprofessional should be able to identify their own personal learning needs. This is not as easy as it sounds. It is not simply a matter of giving everyone what they want or whatever seems easiest. It will take some self-reflection and some trial-and-error investigations for you to identify what really works for you. Some teachers feel they learn best when they receive an outline of the presentation, but research shows that this results in a more passive approach to the information and yields less learning than when teachers have to actively process the information and write notes by hand (Mueller & Oppenheimer, 2014).

Another misconception has arisen from the popular articles claiming that people need learning presentations that match their set "learning styles." We now know that neither adults nor children are truly set as "visual learners" or "kinesthetic learners." People learn in all modalities, depending on their mood, experience, and the content of the information itself. A thorough review by Pashler, McDaniel, Roher, and Bjork (2008) concluded that there was no credible evidence that learning is facilitated by matching content delivery methods to perceived learning style of any individual. This means the best approach is to offer learning content in several formats and focus more on allowing teachers to work on learning the information individually or together until each one has learned what they need to know to change practices. Consider the following questions to start thinking about the kinds of learning that work best for you:

- ◆ Do you like to attend workshops or learn on your own?
- ◆ If given the option to learn on your own, do you usually complete the learning task in the time allotted?
- ◆ Do you like to participate in workshops, or do you prefer to be quiet?
- ◆ Do you retain most from reading articles? Books? Listening to brief podcasts? Viewing 90-minute webinars? Taking graduate courses? Learning via social media?
- ◆ Do you write notes or type on a computer or tablet?
- ◆ Do you have experience learning together with a colleague who can support you and be supported by you?
- ◆ Have you responded well to the coaching model of professional improvement?
- ◆ Do you appreciate attending seminars or presentations during the summer months when you are more relaxed, or do you prefer to do your professional learning during the school year?

Use these questions to identify what are your preferred ways of accessing information and using the information you have learned. You must also begin to understand how you will access, retain, and use information that is presented in a way that is not your preference. Once each person is able to articulate their needs and preferences, it is the job of the supervisor and/or committee to determine how they can provide the same information in different formats with the goal of making sure every staff member who needs the information gets it. The goal must be extended to describe how the team will observe classrooms or try other means to determine that the information is being used.

Changing Practice by Focusing on Teachers as Collaborators

We often hear from teachers of young children that feel isolated in their work. They feel as if their classroom is an island and they have to plan, decorate, adapt, and implement everything on their own. With the growing focus on differentiated instruction throughout the field, working alone to meet the needs of each unique child can seem especially daunting. Professional development does not always mean that you have to personally learn everything needed to teach so many diverse young learners. Another way to meet your goals is to collaborate with others in the field and involve them in your work. Collaborations can make it possible for you to effectively meet the needs of individual learners within the UDL framework. Rather than thinking, "How can I get this job done?" you can shift to thinking "What will it take to get this job done?" Here are some strategies for you to consider:

◆ Collaborating with coaches and mentors for job-embedded professional development means learning within the context of your particular classroom, curriculum, and students about strategies to enhance your teaching practices. It is the best way, but not the only way, to participate in personalized professional development that is just for you. Much has been written about how to make the best use of both roles in the coach/teacher relationship that emphasizes a shared responsibility for sharing and learning (Jablon, Dombro, & Johnsen, 2015).

◆ Co-teaching models enable two educators with different skill sets to work together toward the goal of meeting the educational needs of each individual student. This might involve pairings like general education/special education, general education/English as a second language education, ESL/special education, or English-speaking/Spanish-speaking teachers. Effective co-teaching requires a different approach to planning, talking, and teaching in the early childhood classroom, which is rarely covered in teacher education coursework. When this strategy is adopted, a school or program should offer extensive in-service professional development and ongoing support to make it work. Co-teaching partners need clear guidelines, assignment of responsibilities, and regular planning opportunities.

◆ Collaborative planning can support both co-teaching and independent teaching models. All teachers can benefit from sharing ideas for lessons, activities, and adaptations, especially

when the focus is on updating practice to
support differentiated learning for students
from different experiences, cultures, abilities,
and languages. Planning in isolation often leads
to many duplicated efforts and is usually less
efficient than collaborative planning. In groups,
teachers brainstorm together, inspire creativity
in each other, and benefit from the contributions
each teacher brings from their own unique
experiences, cultures, abilities, and languages.

◆ Specialists such as speech-language pathologists,
ESL teachers, and occupational therapists can be
especially effective when they consult with the
early childhood classroom teacher to support
interventions that can be embedded into each
child's school experience all day every day. For
young children, supports need to be in place at all
times since they are not able to remember and use
strategies provided in occasional pullout lessons.
When specialists work in consultation with you
as the classroom teacher, they not only provide
interventions for a particular child, but they also
build your knowledge and skills that you can use
with many children going forward. If a specialist
pulls a child out to work on a skill or strategy, the
classroom teacher will never see it and will never
be able to repeat it in the regular classroom.

◆ Collaboration with specialists gives you access
to other points of view, research-based strategies
from other fields, and a wider variety of teacher
preparation and practice. Not only do they
bring expertise in their field of specialty, but
they also have learned different ways to present
information, to create materials, and to work with

colleagues. All these experiences can become part of your experience when you collaborate and work actively together instead of turning to other work while a specialist is working with one of your children.

◆ Collaborating with families is another way to build your capacity to meet learning goals for each child. Families have so much information to share about the child's experiences, culture, abilities, and language. When you build relationships with individual families, you can leverage that knowledge to inform your practices at school and to extend the learning you want to see at home. Treat parents as equal partners in a child's educational experience to achieve your desired outcomes. The better informed and supported they are, the more they can add to the work you want to do.

◆ Collaborating with volunteers will open more diverse pathways to information and support. Bilingual volunteers can visit your classroom to read, talk, or play with children in their home languages. Volunteers from the community can bring the richness of their personal talents as well as their culture and experience to build strong connections with children and families in your school or program. It is important to respect diverse volunteers, but part of that respect involves communicating clear expectations about their participation. All volunteers, whether family members or members of the community, need some kind of training and support to ensure their work with young children is appropriate and effective.

Professional Development via Social Media

Social media is a relatively new addition to the professional development scene, but educators have discovered many ways to use these formats to meet personal learning goals. The most attractive feature is that you can access information in any way at any time that meets your personal needs. The interactive component of social media adds that potential for active learning that is so important to adults. Social media gives teachers, administrators, and specialists access to information they might otherwise miss. You don't have to pay for memberships in every relevant organization because social media gives you a way to connect with their specialized information that might help you in your work. If you can't attend a conference, you can follow the hashtag on Twitter to see highlights and links. If you don't subscribe to a journal or magazine, you can often gain access to articles via the organization's Facebook page.

LinkedIn groups are available for many topics related to early childhood education such as ELLs/DLLs in Early Childhood, ALSC (Association for Library Services for Children), or Head Start Professionals. This is a good place to see new posts and articles shared by peers along with lengthy comments and multi-turn discussions. Twitter is a place to post briefly about links, images, or thoughts and to participate in online 140-character chats such as #earlyed, #SLPchat for speech-language pathologists, and #ELLCHAT for discussions on topics about English learners. Other forms of online learning may fall into the category of social media when they invite comments and discussion. These may include podcasts and blogposts. Instagram and Voxer are other ways teachers communicate with each other to share ideas and questions. Social media support the UDL approach to professional development because they make it possible for you to get what you need when you need it. You can ask a question at dawn or midnight and someone will be online to give you an answer. You can get a glimpse inside parts of the field that you haven't seen, and you can build a personal learning network of colleagues near and far. Social media platforms put learning at your fingertips, but it is up to you whether you access that learning in a passive or active way.

Here are the principles of adult learning from Malcolm Knowles that address the ways adults engage in the act of learning (Knowles, et al, 2015):

Adults will experience new learning through the lens of their prior knowledge and experiences

This can be accomplished in two ways. The presenter of the information can plan it in such a way as to ensure the new information is connected to previously covered topics. The learner can also take responsibility for seeking connections to what they already know through active participation in the learning process. Imagine that you are attending a workshop by an out-of-state presenter who shares some fun math activities you could use with your preschoolers. Now imagine how much more meaningful that information would be if the presenter took the time to find out about the curriculum your school is using and she tailored the information with specific examples based on what you already learned about your curriculum. Now think about how much more you could use the information if you took the time to ask the presenter for specific examples based on your own experiences. This is how both the presenter and the learner can use this adult learning principle to change the outcome of a professional learning experience.

This principle can also apply to the ways you read books, listen to podcasts, or even have conversations with colleagues during planning times. Look for supports such as guiding questions or questions for discussion that are provided with professional learning materials to help you prepare to connect with your prior learning.

Professional development providers can use pre-session surveys to build connections with potential learners. By asking meaningful questions about topics to be covered in upcoming presentations, surveys get the audience to start thinking about the prior knowledge they will bring to the professional development. Responses also help the presenter to tailor content and approaches to provide more personalized content and presentation styles.

Adults need environments that make them feel ready to learn

Adults learn best when they are comfortable . . . but not *too* comfortable. Here are some elements that support active learning:

- ◆ Plan comfortable environments, clothing, temperatures, lighting, and sound to help you acquire and retain information.
- ◆ Feeling ready to learn means feeling able to focus your attention on learning for sufficient periods, with any kind of medium. In workshops and courses, move to the front of the room. Let presenters know if you have trouble hearing or if people around you are causing distractions. If reading before bed puts you to sleep, find another time of day.

◆ Seek opportunities for professional learning where you feel comfortable asking questions, exploring more information, and expressing your own processing of the information. Coaching, workshops, and peer discussions should not be intimidating.

Adults also need experiences that make them feel ready to learn
Learning isn't always easy, but it should always give you something you didn't have before and something you can use in your work. While fun and laughter make a learning experience temporarily enjoyable, they don't often result in lasting change or sustained knowledge. It is important to have experiences that are enjoyable but that also lead to improvement of some kind so as not to waste your valuable time. Seek learning experiences that involve you as an active learner by engaging in online or in-person discussions, by taking notes, and by taking time to think about how the content can actually be used in your work. Feeling ready to learn also depends on your actions. Scan the agenda before a meeting. Read the preface of a new book. An independent learner prepares for a learning experience to take charge of their own readiness. Here are the elements of DECAL that help an adult learner experience active learning according to their individual needs.

Guidance for Professional Development Providers

DECAL: Professional Development Actions to Meet the Needs of Adult Learners from Different Life Experiences
Whether you are providing presentations, materials, or interactions to support the professional development of early childhood educators, consider the following

elements of DECAL. Within the UDL framework, these considerations can support effective practices.

Professional Development Tips!

- ◆ Learn about the experiences of your audience before writing professional development content or presenting information. Use examples, wording, and images the audience can relate to.
- ◆ Don't assume anything about the members of your audience. It is always better to get to know them before you provide information by survey, conversations with administrators, and learning more about their school or program.
- ◆ Take responsibility for establishing writing contracts, presentation contracts, or course assignments, requiring enough advance information to allow you to tailor your work to meet the needs of individuals.
- ◆ Consider the experiences of readers and audiences within the context of the federal, state, and local regulations they must follow, the constraints of their curriculum, and the rules of their funding. A presenter might be accustomed to recommending push-in supports for children with disabilities, but that will not meet the learning needs of teachers in a district that requires pullout services due to lack of space.
- ◆ Adult learners are also affected by experiences beyond the workplace. A teacher in a

(continued)

(continued)

> high-intensity urban area might respond differently to some presentation styles than a teacher from a rural area. Some teachers have graduate degrees; others have not attended college. Their behavior with regard to professional learning will be influenced by these types of experiences, and each of them needs to reach learning goals in different ways.

DECAL: Professional Development Actions to Meet the Needs of Adult Learners from Different Cultural Backgrounds

As with considerations about different experiences, adult learners also need to feel a cultural connection based on their life outside the school. Professional development providers and writers, including peer learners and local mentors or coaches, need to get to know elements of each learner's culture. It is not enough to look at learners as members of large cultural groups based on assumptions. Cultural connections are only effective when they come from knowledge about what is meaningful to each individual.

Professional Development Tips!

- ◆ It may not always be possible to learn about the individual cultures of each adult learning reader or participant. Try to include a variety of cultural connections in the examples and content you provide.
- ◆ Avoid the trap of trying so hard not to offend anyone that you provide content that is culturally empty. Cultural connections depend on taking risks to build authentic relationships.

◆ Remember that the goal is to provide information that adult learners relate to. It is not useful to insert random cultural factors or too many cultural factors just for the sake of appearing to respect diversity.

DECAL: Professional Development Actions to Meet the Needs of Adult Learners with Different Abilities

When goals for professional development are viewed through the UDL lens and the focus is on ensuring changes in practice, the abilities of the adult learners must be taken into account. The UDL philosophy is about empowering learners and respecting what makes each learner unique. Some instructors, authors, and administrators worry that adapting for adults with different experiences or abilities could be perceived as "babying" the adult learner by oversimplifying or catering to their needs. This is certainly a challenging issue, but keeping their eyes on the goal of causing change in teaching practice can help. Another way to address this concern is to make advanced learning a learning goal in itself. Program administrators can work with their staff to develop their skills for critical reading, increase their English skills and reading levels, provide direct guidance on the kinds of notetaking, interacting, and attention behaviors expected during presentations, and improve their expressive abilities.

Professional Development Tips!

◆ Don't attribute lack of understanding to a participant's inability to learn. Assume that your goal is to try different pathways until you find a way that helps them learn.

(continued)

(continued)

◆ It is possible to use shorter sentences and simpler vocabulary while maintaining the integrity of the learning content.

◆ Develop collections of meaningful visual cues and video examples to enhance learning.

◆ Provide multiple check-ins to give adult learners feedback on how well they are picking up on content or skills from attending or reading.

◆ Encourage learners to be more aware of their abilities that help them learn or that require adaptations rather than pretending everyone is the same.

◆ With learners of varying abilities, it is critical to eliminate excess words, distracting images, and graphics to stick to key points.

DECAL: Professional Development Actions to Meet the Needs of Adult Learners from Different Languages

Adapting professional development for learners who speak different languages may seem simple, but the reality is these adaptations require more effort than just hiring a translator.

Professional Development Tips!

◆ The first priority should be to encourage bilingual adults to access learning through materials and presentations in their home language. When adults are able to use the language they find most comfortable for learning, they comprehend more and are able to build a stronger foundation of knowledge that can then be transferred to English.

◆ Hire certified translators and interpreters when possible. Look for translators who have some background in early childhood education so they are able to accurately translate professional terms.

◆ Use online resources in the languages of participants. The Language Castle (www. LanguageCastle.com) website has a list of early childhood education professional development resources available in Spanish. The Head Start ECLKC technical assistance website has an English/Spanish toggle button making it easy to access professional learning information in both languages.

◆ Professional development may also be provided in English, but when bilingual adults have a chance to build prior knowledge in their home language, they are better prepared to process and retain learning in English.

◆ Build same-language professional learning networks to make it easier for colleagues to actively process their learning in discussions with peers.

◆ Allow bilingual adults to express their learning in ways that do not depend on their use of their second language. They might demonstrate their learning via role playing, video recording, or writing. Instead of placing the burden on the participant to translate his learning into the provider's language, consider taking on the responsibility of using software or hiring a translator for this purpose.

UDL—Engagement

A fair amount of responsibility rests with an educational professional to be an engaged and motivated learner. Not every presentation will be fun or humorous. Not every video will move as quickly or as slowly as you might like. When you know you need information to do your job well, you need to find a way to engage actively in the learning. It is as much the responsibility of a teacher to get sufficient sleep at night as it is for the presenter or discussion group not to put them to sleep. Be prepared to take notes, ask questions, and think about how new information applies to your practice. When your mind is actively engaged in the information being discussed, presented, or read, your learning is much more effective.

We have overheard teachers at conferences saying things like, "I always go to the challenging behavior workshops" or "I hate those math workshops because I'm not good at math." When there is a choice, many adults will choose a topic or event that fits their comfort level or their current interests. Could you choose a topic that you're not comfortable with because that's the thing you need to learn the most? When you get a new issue of an education journal, do you just read the articles on your favorite topics or do you also take advantage of the articles on topics that are not your favorites but are needed to meet program-wide goals?

In an article about her research on the development of a "growth mindset," Carol Dweck (2015) found that adults can often achieve higher learning goals by changing their approach to learning. She found that learners who take on a growth mindset believe that learning is possible if they try different strategies, and this often results in improved learning outcomes. But Dweck recommends that adult learners should acknowledge it is also true they are better at some things than they are at others, as each adult has different abilities as well as different beliefs about those abilities. So, for example, a teacher that believes she is not good at math might avoid learning new ways to use math in her classroom. But if she could change her view of math learning, and find that she can help children discover math in everyday activities like snack time and outdoor games, she would feel that she is good at teaching math. This kind of change is likely to lead to improvements in teacher practice and in student outcomes. Being proactive and seeking out professional learning opportunities in the areas that are not your favorites can result in the greatest change in your teaching success. It can be helpful to work with your peers to set up professional development that meets individual needs but also satisfies a unifying goal for the program.

What information can help you draft an individual professional development plan? Student outcome data or classroom evaluation scores can provide some guidance about areas in need of improvement, but they don't always tell the whole story. Sometimes, we just like to follow a particular author or blogger, or a friend recommends a new book we hadn't thought of reading before. True growth in a professional field calls for both formal and informal encounters with new information that keep us thinking and improving practice, and enjoying our work.

Guidance for administrators often recommends that professional development goals should be planned with each individual teacher and staff member. Some administrators worry that not every teacher recognizes areas in which they need improvement, or that there may be some program-wide content that everyone needs to learn whether they request it or not. These are valid concerns. As a self-determining professional learner, each of us has to allow that there are some things we have to learn that we did not necessarily choose to learn. The UDL approach provides some answers to this dilemma, but prepares both the administrator and the teacher to think more intentionally about the way that information is delivered and acted upon.

Here are the principles of adult learning from Malcolm Knowles that address the factors that make learning engaging (Knowles et al., 2015):

Adults need to understand why they need to learn new information
From both the learner's and the presenter's point of view, this principle is very important. Work in partnership with other colleagues and administrators to set clear goals so that all professional learning helps you take steps toward those goals. Adult learning goals should be about changing educator behaviors, not just about increasing knowledge. Make the goals measurable and meaningful to your work.

Adults need to see themselves as effective, self-directed learners
Self-determination is the critical feature of this component.

Adults learn best when the new knowledge is focused on solving a problem they need to solve
Setting goals that are measurable and meaningful for your work will help you see learning as a means to an end.

Adult learning is especially affected by the individual's level of
motivation and belief that the new knowledge
will be useful to them

This principle refers to your ability to clearly see what
this new knowledge will mean to your own work, rather
than just believing it is important to early childhood
education in general.

Guidance for Professional Development Providers

DECAL: Professional Development Engagement to Meet the Needs of Adult Learners with Different Life Experiences

Professional development presenters and writers should
think of engagement in terms of the principles of adult
learning described above. Engagement is not a synonym
for entertainment. To be effective, professional development should respect adults as self-directed learners and
help them see the value of the learning for their work.
This requires knowing something about the experiences
and beliefs of your audience of learners so you can support their growth as individuals. Not every teacher has
had experiences that make self-directed learning a habit
for them. Not every reader or participant will immediately
recognize the purpose you envision for the content you
provide. Addressing these differences will enhance the
effectiveness of each type of professional development.
These factors should also be considered by administrators
as they cultivate a community of lifelong learners who are
prepared and motivated to learn. Here are some strategies
to help.

Professional Development Tips!

◆ Use surveys, research, or informal conversations to learn about the experiences of your audience so you can connect with their individual learning needs. If, for example, a principal tells you his teachers always respond best to "make and take" workshops, that doesn't mean you have to present a make and take workshop. It means that you have to know that about the experience of your audience so you can be explicit in making the connection to your content.

◆ Humor can be an effective tool for engagement, but the experiences of the participants will affect how each of them reacts to humorous expressions. Be observant about participant responses and be prepared to change course accordingly.

◆ Adult learners often approach professional development with preconceived notions based on prior experiences. These can be hard to undo in a short period. Presenters can work with educational leaders to uncover negative assumptions and help to work toward more positive attitudes before professional development begins.

◆ Because of differences in previous experiences, it is not always possible to make changes so that one professional development resource or presentation works for everyone.

Think instead about the goals to be accomplished and the variety of professional development resources needed to get all staff to those goals.

◆ Professional learning takes true commitment from the learner, the employer, and the provider. All three components of this partnership must take responsibility for meeting the engagement needs of adult learners. Whether on a small scale or large scale, in person or remote, professional development will be more successful with collaborative pre-planning and implementation supports.

DECAL: Professional Development Engagement to Meet the Needs of Adult Learners from Different Cultural Backgrounds

Considerations about the cultural backgrounds of adult learners are similar to considerations about the experiences of learners. Culture is part of each adult learner's experience that might influence how they tackle their own professional development and how they respond to reading, listening, and discussing. These tips will assist you in addressing these factors.

Professional Development Tips!

◆ Encourage readers and participants to engage in self-reflection about cultural factors

(continued)

(continued)

that might come into play when accessing professional learning, and invite them to share to inform providers. Ask about factors such as

- o comfort with questioning authority figures
- o comfort communicating disagreements
- o adherence to time schedules
- o speaking up in large group settings
- o willingness to participate in role playing or demonstrations that involve touching others
- o comfort with certain slang or expressions
- o assumptions about early childhood education and adult education developed while growing up in another country.

DECAL: Professional Development Engagement to Meet the Needs of Adult Learners with Different Abilities

Different abilities affect how a person will access and use new information, but they also influence the feelings people have about engaging in professional learning. Supporting different pathways to learning for adults with different abilities will enhance their engagement. Even though Carol Dweck (2015) encouraged educators to overcome the emotional limits they place on their learning through negative self-talk, she also acknowledged that sometimes, different abilities will limit learning. The key is to find a balance that encourages learners to stretch themselves to go beyond their perceived limits while supporting their learning within those existing limits.

Professional Development Tips!

- Provide plenty of time for learning to take root for those who need it, but offer enrichment and advancement activities for those who are ready to move on.
- Offer multiple modalities and pathways of learning to ensure all participants can progress in their learning. Within an article, that might include vignettes, summary tables, and narrative. For workshops, that might include lecture, discussion, and demonstrations.
- Break learning down into smaller chunks so each accomplishment is noticeable and supports engagement in the next step.

DECAL: Professional Development Engagement to Meet the Needs of Adult Learners from Different Languages

Connecting learning with the languages of the learners contributes to engagement.

Professional Development Tips!

- Take translation seriously. Poor quality translations may cause participants to feel disrespected and disengaged.
- Invite learners to be active participants in the translation process to help them take ownership of the role their language plays in their own learning.

(continued)

(continued)

◆ If you present information in different languages, ask for feedback in those languages, too.

Addressing Critical Professional Learning Topics with a UDL Approach

There are many demands placed on early childhood educators today. That means there are many things they have to learn about, and that learning must result in changes in practice. The support of the UDL approach can significantly improve the chances of success for any new rollout. Professional development providers, writers, administrators, and practitioners can all work together to achieve common professional learning goals in ways that include each individual adult learner. When states have introduced Common Core and state standards, the way the information was delivered had a lot to do with how effective their implementation rates were across each state. States like Connecticut (www.ct.gov/oec/cwp/view.asp?a=4541&q=536726) and Illinois (www.illinoisearlylearning.org) support different pathways to learning about standards. Head Start introduced its new early childhood outcomes framework with a toolkit of support resources to enhance implementation (www.eclkc.ohs.acf.hhs.gov/hslc/hs/sr/approach/elof).

Other areas of national and local interest have faced challenges to implementation that might have been helped if the UDL approach to supporting all learners played a bigger role. Examples include kindergarten entry assessments and national standardized assessments. When initiatives like these are introduced without sufficient considerations for diverse adult learners, weakened implementation can have catastrophic consequences. In the field of preschool education, classroom and teacher assessments like ECERS-3, ELLCO, and CLASS yield scores that can affect job security and program funding. Preparing practitioners to understand what is expected in high-quality classrooms depends on how well the plans can be adapted for the different needs of adult learners.

Every early childhood curriculum company should be held accountable for meeting the needs of diverse children who come from Different Experiences, Cultures, Abilities, and Languages. It is just as important that the support materials and professional development they provide should have adaptations for the diversity of adult learners. Curriculum elements, such as meaningful planning for the use of technology and digital resources, should also be considered. As our field changes and evolves, success depends on supporting each member of the early childhood education community along the evolution process. When programs fully adopt the UDL framework to meet the needs of children, families, and educators from Different Experiences, Cultures, Abilities, and Languages with a focus on the most important goals for all, they will achieve the kind of outcomes that will make all early education the success it was meant to be.

7

What Administrators Need to Know

Using the UDL Framework Across the DECAL— Elements to Improve Outcomes for Teachers and Students

Message to Administrators

The intended audience of this book is classroom teachers of children from preschool through grade 3, but we know that real change in teaching practice cannot be accomplished without informed collaboration and support from administrators. Our goal for Chapter 7 is to provide critical information that you need as an administrator of an early childhood education program and to provide it in a way that will make your job easier and more effective. Rest assured that UDL is not a new curriculum to add to your to-do list. It is a way to improve knowledge and practice proactively to bring higher levels of success to any curriculum.

Guided Questions

- ◆ What barriers are you encountering that make it difficult for your school to achieve the level of outcomes you aim for?
- ◆ What federal, state, and funding requirements are pushing you to seek change in your school?
- ◆ What is the aspect of your job in which you feel you are most successful?

Defining Key Terms

We recap the explanations provided earlier for teachers to give administrators an equal footing as we begin our message to you.

1. *Universal Design for Learning (UDL)* is a framework that helps all teachers in all classrooms adapt to meet the needs of each individual child. While the Center for Applied Special Technology (CAST) has started a great movement to use this approach for children with disabilities, we are expanding the framework to work with all students.

2. *Developmentally Appropriate Practice (DAP)* is an approach that focuses on supporting the learning of each individual young child according to his or her interests and level of development. Materials from the NAEYC list the three key considerations of DAP as

    - ◆ knowing about child development and learning,
    - ◆ knowing what is individually appropriate, and
    - ◆ knowing what is culturally appropriate.

3. *DECAL* is a guide for preparing all teachers to meet the needs of children with Different Experiences, Cultures, Abilities, and Languages.

It is a way to focus professional learning and preparation that addresses

- **Experiences** (family income, home literacy practices, stress and trauma, safe environments, health and physical development supports, early care and education, etc.)
- **Culture** (family, community, home country, traditions)
- **Abilities** (gifted, individual learning strengths/abilities/potentials, identified or potential disabilities, mental health issues)
- **Languages** (frequently occurring or rare languages, multiple languages).

And why are these things important to you as an administrator? Because they are explicitly required under the Every Student Succeeds Act of 2015 (ESSA, 2015). According to the CAST (2016) website, UDL is specifically mentioned in ESSA in the following section:

- SEC. 1005. State Plans: States need to show that they have, in consultation with local education agencies, developed and implemented high-quality student assessments, including alternate assessments for students with the most significant disabilities, "using the principles of universal design for learning."
- SEC. 1204. Innovative Assessment and Accountability: States must also develop innovative assessment systems that are accessible to all students and provide accountability to the state standards by "incorporating the principles of universal design for learning."
- SEC. 2221(b)(1). Comprehensive Literacy Instruction: Defined as systematic instruction that

provides practice in reading and writing across the curriculum that "incorporates the principles of universal design for learning."

◆ SEC. 4104. State Use of Funds (for Student Support and Academic Enrichments): Federal education funds under the ESSA must be used by local schools to improve their ability to "use technology, consistent with the principles of universal design for learning, to support the learning needs of all students, including children with disabilities and English learners."

UDL is included in regulations and guidelines in a growing number of states, including New Jersey and Maryland. National leadership organizations such as ASCD (Goodwin & Hein, 2017), National Association for Elementary School Principals (Brown, Tucker, & Williams, 2012) and American Speech-Language-Hearing Association (Ralabate, 2011).

The goal of our book is to support this national leadership and to expand implementation to encourage a more unified, accessible approach to education for all children and all educators.

Change Happens; Be Proactive

One of the most helpful yet untraditional features of UDL is the notion that change in education should be proactive rather than reactive. Why not make your building entrance a ramp so everyone can get in, rather than building stairs and then having to tear them down when they become a barrier to someone in the school community? And, similarly, why choose a curriculum that only offers materials in written English, then spend more money to create props, translations, and other adaptions as new students find that they are not able to access the content. As an administrator, you can guide your staff, families, volunteers, and vendors along the path of proactively creating a learning environment that has the fewest barriers and the greatest potential for success. It takes leadership to support educators as they transition away from outdated but familiar methods such as lecturing, large group instruction, and worksheets. Differentiation and personalized learning have been talked about for years. UDL through the lens of DECAL gives you a way to make personalized planning and learning more manageable for your teachers.

Promising Trends to Watch

Some states are specifically writing UDL into their regulations, and more states are likely to follow. As an example, Maryland posted the Maryland Universal Design for Learning Regulation (COMAR 13A.03.06) in 2013, stating that

> Universal Design for Learning (UDL) means a research-based framework for curriculum design that includes goals, methods, materials and assessments to reduce barriers to learning by providing students multiple accessible support options for
>
> ◆ acquiring information and knowledge;
> ◆ demonstrating knowledge and skills in alternative forms of action and expression; and
> ◆ engaging in learning.
> (Montgomery County Schools, 2016)

They also provide an introductory puppet-based video to explain UDL and an interactive digital learning resource on their learning links website. Just as UDL is a progressive new approach to teaching, some organizations are creating progressive ways to learn about UDL.

Another promising trend is the increase in venues to share strategies and resources via websites and social media, such as:

- ◆ CAST (the Center for Applied Special Technology, www.CAST.org)
- ◆ The UDL Center (www.udlcenter.org) also has Twitter handle, Facebook page, and other social media connections. Their YouTube channel provides several free videos for educators (www. youtube.com/c/udlcenterorg)
- ◆ Twitter chat about UDL: #UDLchat
- ◆ DECAL blog (www.languagecastle.com)
- ◆ UDL has a significant presence on Pinterest with some pages hosted by practitioners and others hosted by authors and experts like this one by Katherine McClaskey (www.pinterest.com/ kmcclaskey/universal-design-for-learning/)
- ◆ LinkedIn lists 45 groups dedicated to Universal Design.

And there are many books, authors, and trainers available. All of these connections help to emphasize that UDL is rising and spreading more thoroughly than a simple fad.

Making the Commitment to Operating the Best Program You Can for Each and Every Child

Highlighting UDL classrooms and practices that support the components of DECAL offers administrators the opportunity to uncover the methods and materials needed to help every child in their program progress and learn. These methods are not derived from magic or mystery. They are common-sense approaches to make learning work for all of the diverse children in your program, using the resources, assets, curriculum, and materials available to your program.

Establishing a Vision for Leading with Diversity in Mind

What is your personal mission? What is your vision for your professional career in the next five years? What is the mission or vision statement of your school? And do any of these statements really guide your behavior or your work? Recently, it has become trendy for schools and districts to post "mission statements" that often result from lengthy team meetings. These statements say things like:

- ◆ XYZ School shall do whatever it takes for every student to achieve high academic standards.
- ◆ XYZ School, in partnership with family and community, will provide all students with numerous and varied opportunities to gain the knowledge and skills necessary to grow into healthy, productive citizens equipped for lifelong learning.
- ◆ XYZ school professionals understand that each student is a unique individual and we are ready to support every student in the pursuit of learning. Our strategies are not limited to rote memorization or text reading. Our purpose is to reach every student in our care.

We often wonder why so much work is put into these statements when they all sound so similar. Does having a mission statement like this really influence changes in practice? Perhaps it is time to establish a vision that says more explicitly that all teachers, para-professionals, and specialists are expected to prepare and implement instruction that meets the needs of each student from different experiences, cultures, abilities, and languages, using the proactive UDL framework to guide planning, designing, and presenting learning experiences.

Meeting the Needs of Each Individual Staff Member

Some universities, such as The William Paterson University of New Jersey where Pam is currently an assistant professor, include course content on UDL. That will help future teachers and staff, but your job is to support the teachers, specialists, paraprofessionals, and volunteers that are already on your staff. Details for making that possible are provided in Chapter 6 of this book. We make the case for the importance to taking into account the different experiences, cultures, abilities and languages of all of the members of your school community as you plan events, professional development, meetings, and communications. The UDL approach is closely aligned with the principles of adult education.

Self-Check

Supporting Teachers, Specialists, and Paraprofessional in Becoming a Universally Designed School

Multiple Means of Representation in the Classroom
- ◆ Have you provided the same information a few different ways (e.g., seeing, hearing, touching) in order for every child to be able to perceive what you are trying to teach?

- ◆ Can the information be presented in the different languages the children speak?
- ◆ Are the symbols you are using in the classroom understood by everyone? How can you teach what the symbol means?
- ◆ Are your directions and expressions understood by everyone? How can you teach what your directions and expressions mean?
- ◆ Do the children in your classroom have the prior knowledge they need to comprehend what you are teaching? If not, how do you provide it?
- ◆ Have you used multiple examples that highlight the skills or knowledge you want to teach?

Multiple Means of Action and Expression in the Classroom

- ◆ Are you providing a way for each child to be able to physically access and manipulate the materials and spaces in the classroom as independently as possible?
- ◆ Are children able to express what they know in many different ways? Are you permitting children to draw, use manipulatives, or even act out what they know?
- ◆ Do children have a fluent way to communicate with us and with their peers?
- ◆ Are you providing the correct level of assistance the children need? Independence is key, and you need to make sure you are not over-supporting or under-supporting them.

Multiple Means of Engagement in the Classroom

- ◆ What are you doing to make sure you are gaining the attention of the children in our classrooms?

- ◆ Are you providing choices and autonomy in the classroom so children can have choices in what interests them?
- ◆ Are you making sure that the materials and activities in our classrooms are relevant and authentic to the students in the classroom?
- ◆ Are you making sure that the children have the correct level of support from the adults in the room? Not enough supports or too many supports are harmful.
- ◆ Do children have some challenges in the activities but not challenges that would frustrate them?
- ◆ Are you designing the supports children need to reach their personal goals?
- ◆ Are you teaching children what to do when they feel frustrated?
- ◆ Are children seeing and celebrating their own successes?

Resources for Leaders

In this section, we have gathered key resources that meet the particular needs of administrators.

Nemeth, K. (Ed.). (2014). *Young dual language learners: A guide for preK–3 leaders.* Philadelphia, PA: Caslon Inc.

www.naesp.org/principal-septemberoctober-2012-common-core/access-common-core-all-0

www.naesp.org/sites/default/files/Brown_Tucker_Williams_SO12.pdf

www.ascd.org/publications/books/101042/chapters/Making-Universal-Design-for-Learning-a-Reality.aspx

Right from the Start

Schools Are Changing—What Does That Mean to a Teacher?

When we started this book, we wanted you to come to the same conclusion that we did: if we plan to do the same old things, we can't be surprised if we get the same old results. Why? Because nothing is the same as it used to be.

The twenty-first century is a new time, with new advantages and new dilemmas. Not only does the "what" we teach have to change with the times, the "how" we teach has to change too. The advantages for using the UDL framework within a developmentally appropriate program will meet the needs of all young children.

Working from a proactive stance gives us an opportunity to look at each child separately, as well as each group as a whole. There are many different ways to make sure each child gets what they need, without sacrificing what someone else needs. It is essential that teachers have the knowledge and the support to make sure every student is included and succeeds to the best of their ability. With UDL strategies, educators can make it possible for every child to be the best he can be.

References

Ackerman, D., & Tazi, Z. (2015). *Enhancing young Hispanic dual language learners' achievement: Exploring strategies and addressing challenges.* Princeton, NJ: Educational Testing Service.

Al-Azawei, A., Serenelli, F., & Lundqvist, K. (2016). Universal design for learning (UDL): A content analysis of peer reviewed journals from 2012 to 2015. *Journal of the Scholarship of Teaching and Learning 16*(3), 39–56. doi:10.14434/josotl.v16i3.19295

Annie E. Casey Foundation. (2013a). *Early warning confirmed: A research update on third-grade reading.* Baltimore, MD: Author. Retrieved from http://www.aecf.org/resources/early-warning-confirmed/

Annie E. Casey Foundation, (2013b). *The 2015 kids count data book: State trends in child well being.* Retrieved from http://www.aecf.org/resources/the-2015-kids-count-data-book/

August, D., & T. Shanahan, (Eds.). (2008). *Developing reading and writing in second-language learners: Lessons from the Report of the National Literacy Panel on Language-Minority Children and Youth.* New York, NY: Routledge.

Brillante, P. (2017). *The essentials: Supporting young children with disabilities in the classroom.* Washington, DC: National Association for the Education of Young Children.

Burgstahler, S. (2008). *Universal design in education: Principles and applications.* Retrieved from http://www.washington.edu/doit/Brochures/Academics/ud_edu.html

Cambridge International. (2015). *Active learning*. Retrieved from http://www.cie.org.uk/images/271174-active-learning.pdf

Center for Applied Special Technology (CAST). (2016). *UDL in the ESSA*. Retrieved from http://www.cast.org/whats-new/news/2016/udl-in-theessa.html#.V7pdu2WZ6hU

Center for Disease Control and Prevention, Autism and Developmental Disabilities Monitoring Network. (2016). *Community report from the Autism and Developmental Disabilities Monitoring (ADDM) Network*. Retrieved from http://www.cdc.gov/ncbddd/autism/documents/community_report_autism.pdf

Center for Public Education. (2007). *What research says about English language learners: At a glance*. Retrieved from http://www.centerforpubliceducation.org/Main-Menu/Instruction/What-research-says-about-English-language-learners-At-a-glance

Child Trends Databank. (2014). *Dual language learners*. Retrieved from http://www.childtrends.org/?indicators=dual-language-learners

Council for Exceptional Children, Division for Early Childhood (DEC). (2010). *DEC position statement on cultural and linguistic responsiveness*. Missoula, MT: Council for Exceptional Children Division for Early Childhood.

Division of Early Childhood (DEC). (2007). *Promoting positive outcomes for children with disabilities: Recommendations for curriculum, assessment, and program evaluation*. Missoula, MT: Council for Exceptional Children Division for Early Childhood.

Dweck, C. (2015). Carol Dweck revisits the 'growth mindset'. *Education Week 35*(05), 20, 24.

Erikson, E. H. (Ed.). (1963). *Youth: Change and challenge.* New York, NY: Basic Books.

Espinosa, L. (2013). *PreK–3rd: Challenging common myths about dual language learners.* (Pre-K–3rd Policy to Action Brief No. 10). New York, NY: Foundation for Child Development.

Goodwin, B., & Hein, H. (2017). Research matters/learning styles: It's complicated, *Educational Leadership* 74(7), 79–80.

Gross, M. (1999). Small poppies: Highly gifted children in the early years. *Roeper Review* 21(3) 207–2014.

Halle, T. G., Hair, E. C., McNamara, M., Wandner, L., & Chien, N. (2012). Predictors and outcomes of early vs. later English language proficiency among English language learners in the ECLS-K. *Early Childhood Research Quarterly, 27*(1), 1–20.

Houtrow, A. J., Kandyce-Larson, L. M., Olson, P. W., & Newacheck, N. H. (2014). Childhood disability trends, 2000–2010. *Pediatrics.* August 2014. doi:10.1542/peds. 2014–0594

Isaacs, J. (2012). *Starting school at a disadvantage: The school readiness of poor children.* Washington, DC: Brookings Institution.

Jablon, J., Dombro, A., & Johnsen, S. (2015) Coaching with powerful interactions: A guide for partnering with early childhood teachers. Washington, DC: NAEYC.

Kaiser, B., & Rasminsky, J. S. (2016). Challenging behavior in young children: Understanding, preventing and responding effectively (4th ed.). New York, NJ: Pearson.

Karnes, F. A., Manning, S., Besnoy, K., Cukierkorn, J., & Houston, H. (2005). *Appropriate practices for screening, identifying, and serving potentially gifted preschoolers.* Hattiesburg, MS: The Frances A. Karnes Center for Gifted Studies.

Knowles, M. S., Holton, E. F., & Swanson, R. A. (2015). The adult learner: The definitive classic in adult education and human resource development (8th ed.). New York, NY: Routledge.

Livingston, G. (2014). *Fewer than half of U.S. kids today live in a 'traditional' family.* Retrieved from http://www.pewresearch.org/fact-tank/2014/12/22/less-than-half-of-u-s-kids-today-live-in-a-traditional-family/

Magnuson, K. (2013). Reducing the effects of poverty through early childhood interventions *Fast Focus* 17, 2–6.

McWilliam, R. A. & Scott, S. (2001). Integrating therapy into the classroom. *Individualizing inclusion in child care.* Retrieved from http://csd.wp.uncg.edu/wp-content/uploads/sites/6/2012/12/Integrating-Therapy-Into-Classrooms1.pdf

Miller, E., & Almon, J. (2009) *Crisis in the kindergarten: Why children need to play in school.* College Park, MD: Alliance for Childhood.

Montgomery County Schools, MD. (2016). Retrieved from http://www.cast.org/whats-new/news/2016/udl-in-theessa.html#.V7pdu2WZ6hU

Mueller, P., & Oppenheimer D. (2014). The pen is mightier than the keyboard: Advantages of longhand over laptop note taking. *Psychological Science* 25(6), 1159–1168.

Mulvey, J. D., Cooper, B. S., Accurso, K. F., & Garliardi, K. (2014). *Education is special for everyone: How schools can best serve all students.* New York, NY: Rowman and Littlefield.

National Association for the Education of Young Children (2009). *Developmentally appropriate practice in early childhood programs serving children from birth through age 8: A position statement of the National Association for the Education of Young Children.* Washington, DC: Authors.

National Association for the Education of Young Children and National Association of Child Care Resource and Referral Agencies. (2011). *Early childhood education professional development, training and technical assistance glossary.* Washington, DC: NAEYC.

National Association for the Education of Young Children/National Association of Early Childhood Specialists in State Departments of Education. (2003). *Early childhood curriculum, assessment and program evaluation: Position statement with extended resources.* Washington, DC: National Association for the Education of Young Children. Retrieved from https://www.naeyc.org/files/naeyc/file/positions/CAPEexpand.pdf

National Institute for Early Education Research (2016). *The state of preschool 2015.* New Brunswick, NJ: Rutgers University.

National Task Force on Early Childhood Education for Hispanics. (2007). *Para nuestros niños: Expanding and enhancing early education for Hispanics.* Retrieved from www.ecehispanic.org/work/expand_MainReport.pdf

Nemeth, K. (2009). *Many languages, one classroom: Tips and techniques for teaching English language learners in preschool.* Beltsville, MD: Gryphon House.

Nemeth, K. (2011). *Home language vs. English only.* Retrieved from http://www.naeyc.org/event/supporting-dual-language-learners

Nemeth, K. (2012). *Basics of supporting dual language learners.* Washington, DC: National Association for the Education of Young Children.

Nemeth, K., Brillante, P., & Mullen, L. (2017). *Naming the new, inclusive early childhood education: All teachers ready for DECAL!* Retrieved from http://www.languagecastle.com/

Neuman, S. B., & Celano, D. (2012). *Giving our children a fighting chance: Affluence, literacy, and the development of information capital.* New York, NY: Teachers College Press.

Office of Head Start. (2007). *Dual language learning: What does it take?* Washington, DC: Authors.

Opportunity for Independence. (2011). *Dignity of risk.* Retrieved from http://ofiinc.org/dignity-risk-0

Pashler, H., McDaniel, M., Roher, D., & Bjork, R. (2008). Learning styles: Concepts and evidence. *Psychological Science in the Public Interest, 9*(3), 106–119.

Pinkos, M. (2007, October 30). *Welcoming remarks from the deputy of policy,* Office of English Language Acquisition, U.S. Department of Education. Celebrate Our Rising Stars Summit VI, Washington, DC.

Ralabate, P. K. (2011). Universal design for learning: Meeting the needs of all students. *The ASHA Leader, Vol. 16,* 14–17. doi:10.1044/leader.FTR2.16102011.14

Rideout, V., & Katz, V. (2016) Opportunity for all? Technology and learning in low-income families. Joint report from Rutgers University and the Joan Ganz Cooney Center.

Rose, D. H., Harbour, W. S., Johnston, C. S., Daley, S. G., & Abarbanell, L. (2006). Universal design for learning in postsecondary education: Reflections on principles and their application. *Journal of Postsecondary Education and Disability, 19*(2), 17. Retrieved from http://www.udlcenter.org/sites/udlcenter.org/files/UDLinPostsecondary.pdf

Stile, S. W., Kitano, M., Kelley, P., & LeCrone, J. (1993). Early intervention with gifted children: A national survey. *Journal of Early Intervention 17*(1), 30–35.

Tabors, P. O. (2008). *One child, two languages: A guide for early childhood educators of children learning English as a second language* (2nd ed.). Baltimore, MD: Brookes.

Vygotsky, L. S. (1977). Play and its role in the mental development of children, In M. Cole (Ed). *Soviet developmental psychology*. While Plains, NY: M.E. Sharp.

Ziegler, K., & Camarota, S. A. (2016). *61 Million immigrants and their young children now live in the United States*. Washington, DS. Center for Immigration Studies. Retrieved from http://cis.org/61-Million-Immigrants-and-Their-Young-Children-Now-Live-in-the-United-States

Appendix A

Classroom Planning Resource Guide

Tips for finding, choosing, and making materials for the UDL classroom appear throughout the chapters of this book. Here, we have compiled the top tips to make classroom planning easy and accessible.

UDL-ECE Teacher Tips Guide for Choosing Classroom Materials

- ◆ Provide open-ended materials like clay, blocks, and paints that each child can use to express himself at her own level.
- ◆ Small pitchers and serving utensils help all children snack independently.
- ◆ Menus from ethnic restaurants and other real items from the neighborhood support cultural connections.
- ◆ Employ a changeable Picture Exchange Communication System (PECS) for all kinds of communication needs.
- ◆ Provide games giving everyone a chance to test their skill, but not always making everyone win and not always making just the tallest or most advanced students win.
- ◆ Instead of games with thin cards that are hard to pick up, paste the cards on pieces of thick cardboard or foam board for easy handling.

(continued)

(continued)

◆ Add more real items for math, science, and other manipulative activities. Dual language learners get a head start when working with familiar materials that they understand and know about. This is another reason to use socks for sorting games instead of meaningless plastic toys or cutout shapes. Collect items from nature, from kitchens, sports, and so on.

◆ Being culturally responsive also means being respectful about the lives of children who have a variety of advantages and disadvantages—make sure you have books and materials that represent children who may have housing or food instability or who are in foster care with changing arrangements.

◆ Check your books, displays, and games to be sure there are items that are relatable for each child.

◆ Visit thrift stores to collect dress-up items rather than ordering inauthentic items from catalogs. Look for favorite team colors, items related to the work of the families, and relevant pastimes.

◆ Provide gardening materials that every student can use, but avoid sharp implements so all can be safe.

◆ Cultures of the children can be represented in anything from art supplies to music to the plants you choose for the garden and the games you play outdoors.

◆ Plastic and magnetic letters are available in some languages other than English. If you

need other characters, print them out and
glue onto plastic sheets and add magnets.

◆ Provide some kind of bin or locker for
each student to keep a few important items
securely in the classroom.

◆ The Joan Ganz Cooney Center offers a new
website (www.joinkidmap.org). The name
"kidmap" means Kids' Inclusive and Diverse
Media Action Project. In 2017, they developed
the DIG—Diverse and Inclusive Growth—
checklist to identify high-quality apps for
diverse children (www.joinkidmap.org/
digchecklist/). They recommend that a UDL
approach should be used to ensure accessible
functionality and navigation of children's apps.

UDL-ECE Teacher Tips Guide for Finding Classroom Materials

◆ Check local flea markets, yard sales, and thrift
shops for locally and culturally responsive
items.

◆ Ask local charities or cultural organizations to
provide culturally relevant materials.

◆ Materials can be requested by mail from the
embassy representing the home country of
each child.

◆ Ask restaurants and local businesses for
ethnic menus, posters, and other culturally
relevant materials.

◆ Ask family members or volunteers to
contribute print-rich, photo-filled magazines,

(continued)

(continued)

newspapers, and catalogs from different countries.

◆ Borrow from the public library.

◆ Online libraries of digital books or multilingual story apps are good options for hard to find languages.

◆ Ask scout troops or college groups to design adaptations for furniture and equipment.

UDL-ECE Teacher Tips Guide for Creating Classroom Materials

◆ Create class books using photos of the children's actual homes, neighborhoods, and the school community. Think about places the children go such as the grocery store, food bank, park, zoo, homeless shelter, bank, welfare office, clinic, grange center, veterinarian, county fair, street festival, and so on.

◆ Check local flea markets, yard sales, and thrift shops for culturally relevant materials you can use to create centers, projects, activities, and artwork for the classroom.

◆ Provide open-ended materials like clay, blocks, and paints that each child can use to express himself at her own level.

◆ Use family photos glued to boxes and blocks to make relatable people in the block or table toy area.

◆ If your curriculum provides required reading books, create supplemental materials that support the vocabulary and topics in those books with additional images that are culturally relevant to use as puzzles or memory game pieces.

◆ Use photos to create picture schedules all children can follow.

◆ Keep a collection of adaptation materials that can make purchased materials easier to use such as modeling clay, sponge hair curlers, rubber bands, tennis balls, ace bandages, cardboard, foam board, and different types of tape.

UDL-ECE Teacher Tips Guide for Partnering with Families to Update Classroom Materials

◆ Ask families to take pictures of their child's plate at dinner and use the images to create class books or laminate them to serve as pretend food in the dramatic play area. Families can also send in empty food containers that can be cleaned and used here, too.

◆ In the small toy or manipulatives area, replace meaningless plastic items with real items that children see at home. When you teach sorting with a collection of socks, children see the same items at home and can extend their learning in ways that don't happen with plastic school supplies.

◆ Invite families to record themselves as they walk around the room talking about the

(continued)

(continued)

> materials and activities in their primary language. Use the recordings to practice vocabulary you can use with children in their home languages.
>
> ◆ Post videos of upcoming lessons and activities so families can talk with children about what to expect and help to prepare them.
>
> ◆ Involve families in sharing stories, games, and rhymes they remember from their own childhood. They may participate directly in class or contribute recordings that can be used for them.
>
> ◆ Organize a family fix-up day and engage families in working together to repair, paint, clean, and decorate the classroom or playground.

UDL-ECE Teacher Tips Guide for Empowering Students in UDL Classrooms

◆ Use open-ended materials like clay, blocks, and paints that each child can use to express himself and create items that can be used for learning in the classroom.

◆ Provide small pitchers and serving utensils to help all children snack independently.

◆ Give children access to basic necessities such as clean underwear and clothes, toothbrushes and toothpaste, and hairbrushes that they can use to take care of themselves even if those items are not always available in their home.

- Invite the children to be recorded as they talk about the items and displays in the different areas of the classroom in their home languages to help teachers create labels and conversation starters in each language.
- Use labels and name tags that include both visual and tactile cues so all children can operate independently in the classroom.
- Provide story making apps that allow children to create, collaborate, narrate, and share their own stories.
- Use apps that allow children with different levels of dexterity to participate and learn— such as voice activation or paddle-switch simulations.
- Help children learn to help each other rather than always relying on an adult. Every empowered child has something to offer a friend.

Appendix B

Guided Questions

Here are the guided questions from all the chapters. You can use them to prepare assignments, start discussions in staff meetings, post on social media chats for feedback, explore more deeply in a professional learning community, and more.

Chapter 2

- ◆ How do you routinely present information to the students in your classroom? Is it always with visuals? Do you always talk about the topic? How many ways do you present the same information?
- ◆ When do you find it most challenging to communicate with the children in your group?
- ◆ What kind of technology are you most comfortable using that could help you establish multiple means of representation in your classroom?
- ◆ Take a closer look at the items on display in your classroom. How are you presenting information that you want your children to know? Which items are really used to facilitate communication? Which are rarely or never discussed?

Chapter 3

- ◆ Which centers in your classroom are well used by the children and which centers are ignored by the children? Do children stay longer at certain centers and have more complex play with those materials? Do specific children seem to ignore a particular center?

◆ How are the children in your group expressing what they know and can do during activities? Which children are the most challenging for you to know what they can do or interpret what they are trying to show/tell you? What contributes to this challenge?

◆ When you step back and watch the children in child-directed activities, what are they doing? How are they playing and planning what to do? Are they using the skills and knowledge you have taught them in teacher-directed activities? What other skills are they using?

Chapter 4

◆ How much time do children spend together in play?

◆ Do you have times of the day when children must work alone, or they must work in groups? How much flexibility do you offer with that?

◆ How much of your instruction relies on rote learning of concepts such as letters, numbers, colors, and shapes? How much of your instruction is about teaching specific routines that all children must follow? Are there any times when children can figure things out all on their own?

◆ When you step back and just watch, what materials do children show the most interest in? Do you have a way you want children to play or use those materials? Do children have time in the day to explore with those materials any way they want?

Chapter 5

- ◆ How has your program changed over the last five years? How about the past 10 or 15 years?
- ◆ What is the most challenging part of serving the needs of all the children in your program?
- ◆ What barriers have you already faced and what barriers do you expect to face in the near future?
- ◆ What new knowledge do you think the professionals in your program need? What new knowledge do you think you need?

Chapter 6

- ◆ What is the best professional development experience you've had? Can you describe what makes it so memorable?
- ◆ How does your school help you learn from and with your peers?
- ◆ What is your administrator's role in professional development?

Chapter 7

- ◆ What barriers are you encountering that make it difficult for your school to achieve the level of outcomes you aim for?
- ◆ What federal, state, and funding requirements are pushing you to seek change in your school?
- ◆ What is the aspect of your job in which you feel you are most successful?

Taylor & Francis eBooks

Helping you to choose the right eBooks for your Library

Add Routledge titles to your library's digital collection today. Taylor and Francis ebooks contains over 50,000 titles in the Humanities, Social Sciences, Behavioural Sciences, Built Environment and Law.

Choose from a range of subject packages or create your own!

Benefits for you

>> Free MARC records
>> COUNTER-compliant usage statistics
>> Flexible purchase and pricing options
>> All titles DRM-free.

Benefits for your user

>> Off-site, anytime access via Athens or referring URL
>> Print or copy pages or chapters
>> Full content search
>> Bookmark, highlight and annotate text
>> Access to thousands of pages of quality research at the click of a button.

REQUEST YOUR **FREE** INSTITUTIONAL TRIAL TODAY

Free Trials Available
We offer free trials to qualifying academic, corporate and government customers.

eCollections – Choose from over 30 subject eCollections, including:

Archaeology	Language Learning
Architecture	Law
Asian Studies	Literature
Business & Management	Media & Communication
Classical Studies	Middle East Studies
Construction	Music
Creative & Media Arts	Philosophy
Criminology & Criminal Justice	Planning
Economics	Politics
Education	Psychology & Mental Health
Energy	Religion
Engineering	Security
English Language & Linguistics	Social Work
Environment & Sustainability	Sociology
Geography	Sport
Health Studies	Theatre & Performance
History	Tourism, Hospitality & Events

For more information, pricing enquiries or to order a free trial, please contact your local sales team: www.tandfebooks.com/page/sales

Routledge
Taylor & Francis Group

The home of
Routledge books

www.tandfebooks.com